Joseph Jacobs

Barlaam and Josaphat

English lives of Buddha. Edited and induced by Joseph Jacobs

Joseph Jacobs

Barlaam and Josaphat
English lives of Buddha. Edited and induced by Joseph Jacobs

ISBN/EAN: 9783337246686

Printed in Europe, USA, Canada, Australia, Japan

Cover: Foto ©Lupo / pixelio.de

More available books at **www.hansebooks.com**

Barlaam and Josaphat

English Lives of Buddha
Edited and Induced by
Joseph Jacobs

To
JOSEPH JACOBS

BARLAAM AND JOSAPHAT

O friend, who sittest young yet wise
 Beneath the Bô-tree's shade,
Confronting life with kindly eyes,
 A scholar unafraid

To follow thought to any sea
 Or back to any fount,
'Tis modern parables to me
 From thy instruction mount.

Was Barlaam truly Josaphat,
 And Buddha truly each?
What better parable than that
 The unity to preach—

The simple brotherhood of souls
 That seek the highest good;
He who in kingly chariot rolls,
 Or wears the hermit's hood!

The Church mistook? These heathen once
 Among her Saints to range!
That deed of some diviner dunce
 Our wisdom would not change.

For Culture's Pantheon they grace
 In catholic array.
Each Saint hath had his hour and place,
 But now 'tis All Saints' Day.

I. ZANGWILL

OCTOBER 27, 1895

PREFACE

I TRUST I shall not be accused of overstepping the bounds of modesty if I confess from the start that I have chiefly reprinted the accompanying versions of the legend of *Barlaam and Josaphat* in order that I might write the Introduction to them. The English versions of the Barlaam legend are but poor things, contracted and truncated to such an extent that scarcely anything remains of their resemblance to the original. Of the five or six versions extant in English, I have selected that one which first appeared in print, viz., Caxton's treatment in his *Golden Legend*, and the last that appeared in print independently, a Chapbook in verse, kindly placed at my disposal by Mr. G. H. Skipwith.

I have not, however, confined myself to the English versions in the Introduction, which deals generally with the history of the legend, which forms one of the most remarkable episodes in the history of literature. The fact that by its means Buddha had been, if only informally, canonised a Saint of the Church, would be enough to attract attention to it. But many of the parables enframed in the legend have had a history even more remarkable than the legend itself. As is well known, the *Caskets* story of the *Merchant of Venice* is ultimately derived from *Barlaam and Josaphat*.

I have for some time been making rather extensive collections for the Introduction to this work, in order to make it a companion study to my treatment of the *Fables of Bidpai* and *Æsop* in the same series. But all that I have collected, and much more also, has been put together by Dr. Ernst Kuhn in a contribution to the *Abhandlungen* of the Bavarian Academy of Science (Munich, 1893). This is one of those erudite bibliographical monographs in which German scholarship excels; and in all those portions of my Introduction, which deal with the bibliographical aspects of the question, and notably in the pedigree and appendices, I make grateful use of Dr. Kuhn's researches.

PREFACE

I have, however, ventured to differ at times from the conclusions which Dr. Kuhn draws from the elaborate series of scholarly facts which he has brought together in his monograph. In the second of my Appendices I have been able to add here and there some further references beyond those collected by Dr. Kuhn, while I may flatter myself that I have arranged all that he has collected in a form more easy of access to the folk-lore student. I have endeavoured to separate the scaffolding of scholarship from the goodly fabric which the results of recent research has erected with some toil. But in order to do this I have been obliged to relegate to the Appendices several good stories and apologues which I can recommend to the reader. It has been my aim to bring within moderate compass a concise statement of the results already reached about this remarkable legend, with full bibliographical references to the critical discussions, where the student can find exact details on the many points of interest or obscurity with which the whole subject bristles.

JOSEPH JACOBS.

P.S.—Through the kindness of Mr. J. S. Cotton, I have been enabled to see a work on Barlaam published at Calcutta in 1895 as a text-book in English. It contains, curiously enough, the Caxton *Barlaam* which I have also given. It has besides a reprint of the three Middle English legends edited by Dr. Horstmann, as well as an eighteenth century tract. The editor, Dr. K. S. Macdonald, is unacquainted with Kuhn's researches, and devotes his Introduction mainly to disproving the possibility of Christianity having been influenced by Buddhism.

INTRODUCTION

BUDDHA and Christ, it may be said, represent the two highest planes which the religious consciousness of mankind has hitherto reached. Each in his way represents the Ideal of a whole Continent. The aim of Asia has always been To Be, the aim of Europe, To Do. The contemplative Sage is the highest ideal of Asia. Europe pins its faith to the beneficent Saint. Both Ideals, to a modern and decadent world, have lost some of their attractiveness. For Sage we are inclined to read Prig and Bore, and it is considered an appropriate fate for the good young man that he should die early. There is a sense of pose in the attitude of any one who nowadays would set up as Saint or Sage, which irritates us moderns, who do nothing if we do not pose. Besides, the trail of professionalism is over us all, and the Professional Saint (Cleric or Philanthropist), or Professional Sage (Thinker or Professor), is an abomination. Yet while Virtue and Wisdom remain goals of human striving, the Ideals of Christ and the Buddha must retain their attraction.

Diverse as are the aims of the Christian and of the Buddhistic schemes, their methods are remarkably similar. They have a common enemy in what is known in Christian parlance as the World. The pleasures of the senses and the pride of power are the chief forces which deflect men from the paths of Wisdom and of Virtue. Till the New Man comes, who shall synthesise all four Ideals, the Christian-Buddhist plan of Renunciation must remain the necessary prerequisite of salvation.

The similarity of the two schemes extends far beyond their general plan. The legend of the founders presents a remarkable set of parallels—the Annunciation, the Massacre of the Innocents, the Temptation in the Wilderness, the Marriage at Cana, the Walking on the Water, the Transfiguration, find *

---

* The most recent enumeration of these parallels is by Dr. Carus in the *Monist*, October, 1894. Many of them parallels more or less close in the Legend of the Buddha.

Both taught by parables, and in several instances the subject of their parables is the same (*Sower: Prodigal Son: Seed and Soil*). Much of their teaching is similar. The stress laid on the spirit as against the letter, the opposition between riches and spirituality, the inwardness of purity, are equally insisted upon in both systems. The formation of a Brotherhood or Church has been in each case the cause of giving permanent effect to the ideals of the founders, and as is well known even the external* cultus have many points of contact.

It is natural that such marked similarities should give rise to thoughts of the dependence of the later Christian on the earlier Buddhistic system. There was fully time since Alexander's visit to India for some knowledge of Buddhism to percolate Syria. Just as Jesus was entering

---

are discussed in an apologetic sense by Dr. T. S. Berry in the "Donnellan Lectures," *Christianity and Buddhism* (S. P. C. K.).

* The Jesuit missionaries in Tibet were astonished to find many minute similarities between the religious ceremonies of the Lama and of the Pope.

upon his public career, a Buddhistic Sage from India created a great sensation throughout the Hellenistic world by causing himself to be burnt alive at Athens (Strabo, XV. i. 73).* And the fame of this self-immolation must have reached Judea, for Josephus refers to it in a speech which he, following the example of Livy, put in the mouth of Eleazar (*Wars*, VII. viii. 7). But it must be confessed that no other evidence can be adduced of the actual spread of Buddhistic doctrines in Western Asia, and the whole case for the dependence of Christianity on Buddhism would have to be solved on Folklore principles. In other words, till Folklore has become so much of a Science as to be able to discriminate between foreign and independent origin, this question must remain an open one.

But there is one piece of evidence, though of much later date, which has at least a reflex bearing on the question. If we can show that in the fifth or sixth century Buddhistic legends and doctrines percolated as far at least as Syria, and there became inextricably combined with Christian dogmas and legends, it becomes

* See my *Bidpai*, p. xlviii.

more probable that a similar mixture of Buddhism and Judaism had taken place in Babylon or Syria in the first century. Such evidence is afforded, as is now well known, by the Legend of SS. Barlaam and Josaphat, which, beside being one of the curiosities of literature, is thus seen to be of considerable theological importance.

I

THE GREEK BARLAAM

IN the great Menology of the Greek Church, under date August 26, stands the entry [μνήμη] τοῦ ὁσίου Ἰωάσαφ, υἱοῦ Ἀβενὴρ τοῦ βασιλέως.

In the Martyrologium Romanum, under date November 27, stands the entry, "*Apud Indos Persis finitimos (commemoratio) sanctorum Barlaam et Josaphat, quorum actos mirandos sanctus Joannes Damascenus conscripsit.*"

When these entries came into the respective martyrologies is somewhat difficult to say. In the Greek Church it was not till after the tenth century, for the Menology of the Emperor Basilius contains no reference to Joasaph. In the Romish martyrologies the first mention of Josaphat among the Saints was in the Catologus Sanctorum of Peter de Natalibus (ob. 1370). It may be conjectured in the latter case that Barlaam and Josaphat owed their inclusion in the saintly calendar, as in the "Golden Legend" of Jacobus de Voragine, to the popularity of the parables which, as we shall see, were connected with their name. But in any case, the ultimate source of each entry is to be found in the life of the two Saints, attributed to St. John of Damascus. In fact, the Roman martyrology in the form given to it by the great Baronius, and just quoted, expressly states that fact.

It must not be supposed that the inclusion of these names in the lists of the Saints is of equal validity with the formal process known as "Canonisation." It is usually stated in summing up the inquiries on which we are about to enter that "Buddha has been canonised as a Saint of the Catholic Church," and much searching of heart has been caused to earnest Catholics by this statement. But M. Cosquin has conclusively shown in a special article devoted to the subject (*Revue des Questions Historiques*, October, 1880) that there is all the difference in the world between the two processes. Inclusion in the calendar only implies a verdict similar to that of a magistrate's court or a Grand Jury; a *prima facie*

b

case for sainthood has been made out. Before canonisation can be obtained, the searching cross-examination of the *Avvocato del Diavolo* must be triumphantly sustained. Modern scholarship has acted the part of the Devil's Advocate with the result that the next edition of the Roman Martyrology will not, in all probability, contain the names of Barlaam and Josaphat.

But that these mysterious personages have been regarded by clergy and laity as veritable Saints of the Church, there can be no doubt. Sir Henry Yule visited a church at Palermo dedicated "Divo Josaphat."* In 1571 the Doge Luigi Mocenigo presented to King Sebastian of Portugal a bone and part of the spine of St. Josaphat. When Spain seized Portugal in 1580 these sacred treasures were removed by Antonio, the Pretender to the Portuguese crown, and ultimately found their way to Antwerp. On August 7, 1672, a grand procession defiled through the streets of Antwerp, carrying to the cloister of St. Salvator the holy remains of St. Josaphat. There, for ought

---

* It is, however, just possible that this refers to a Polish saint of that name of the seventeenth century.

I know to the contrary, they remain to the present day.

But while Catholic Christendom had no doubt as to the reality of these Saints, Catholic scholarship was by no means positive as to the authorship of the Legend of the Saints. The Greek MSS. attributed it to "John, Monk of the Convent of St. Saba," or St. Sinai. It is only in the latest MSS. that this Monk John is directly identified with John of Damascus, a somewhat distinguished theologian of the eighth century. He was the only ecclesiastical writer of the name of John to whom the book could be attributed, and scholarship, like Nature herself, abhors a vacuum. And so the book of Barlaam and Joasaph has been included among the works of John of Damascus ever since his editors have collected them together. Yet they have not been without their doubts, and they always felt themselves obliged to defend the inclusion of the book. One of his editors indeed, Lequien, went so far as to exclude it altogether from the authentic works. The whole question has been carefully threshed out by M. Zotenberg in his *Notice sur le Livre de Barlaam*

(Paris, 1886). He may fairly be said to have disposed of the claims of John of Damascus. He points out that the style of the book is superior in purity, correctness, and richness to that of the recognised works of John of Damascus. The defenders of the authorship had pointed to similarities of doctrine in ecclesiastical matters in the Barlaam and in the recognised writings of John of Damascus. M. Zotenberg in his case traces the similarity to a common source. Apart, however, from these negative arguments, M. Zotenberg has, by a careful scrutiny of the theology of Barlaam, arrived at an ingenious crucial difference between the views expressed in the book and those known to be held by John of Damascus. Each decade of the earlier centuries of Christianity can be distinguished by its fashionable heresy. The years 620–38 were dominated in Christian theology by the discussion of the exact relations of the human and divine Will in Christ. I do not profess to understand the minutiæ of the discussion, and my readers will probably be grateful to me if I profess the heresy of Lord Dundreary with regard to it. But it seems that the Christian world of the East was divided between Dyotheletism, which recognised two Wills in Christ, and Monotheletism, which fuses the two into one. The decisive moment in the controversy came in 633, when Cyrus of Alexandria promulgated his Nine Articles, by which Monotheletism became incumbent on the orthodox. Now the book of Barlaam is distinctly Dyotheletic in tendency, and by this subtle means we are therefore led by M. Zotenberg to the conclusion that its date must be anterior at least to the year 633. On the other hand, a *terminus a quo* is given for the book by the fact that the Convent of St. Saba was refounded by that Saint in the year 491.

M. Zotenberg went a step further in determining the age of the book by a careful examination of the historical background involved in it. The Religions of the world are stated to be three: Idolatry, Judaism, Christianity. Hence M. Zotenberg infers that the book was written previous to the marvellous spread of Islam in the seventh century. And in the particular form of Idolatry professed by Abenner, King of the Indians and father of Joasaph, clear reference is to be found in the tenets of

Mazdeism under the later Sassanides of Persia. The idolaters are spoken of in the book as Chaldeans, and their faith as worship of the elements. There is a Chief of the Magi referred to, whose relations with the King of the "Indians" exactly corresponds to the position of the supreme Mobed in the Sassanide Kingdom. Grappling more closely with his subject, M. Zotenberg then points out common traits of Abenner and Chosroes the Great of Persia (531–79). Both kings are distinguished by their devotion to duty and to the national faith, and at the same time by their interest in, and inquiries about, competing creeds. It is besides a remarkable fact that Anushzad, son of Chosroes, was imprisoned for a rebellion, for which the motive was mainly religious. Finally, the great disputation between the Magi and the Christians in the Barlaam finds a remarkable parallel in a similar public disputation held *circa* 525 before Kobad, King of Persia, and his son Chosroes. To these arguments of M. Zotenberg, connecting Barlaam with the reign of Chosroes, I would add the fact that it is with his reign that a well-founded tradition associates the first stage westward of the *Fables of Bidpai*, which have so many points of similarity with the Parables of Barlaam.

M. Zotenberg's arguments with regard to the Greek text and its date have been recently reinforced by two remarkable discoveries that have been made with regard to its sources. One of the striking episodes of the book is where Nachor is made to take the place of the holy hermit Barlaam, with the intention that he should make a feeble defence of Christianity in a public disputation between the two faiths which is about to be held before the wavering Josaphat. Nachor is accordingly about to play the part of a "bonnet" or confederate when he is forced by Josaphat to play fair, and accordingly delivers a glowing defence of the Christian Religion which routs his opponents. Changing the venue, the incident might have been taken from one of Capt. Hawley Smart's novels.

It would seem that Nachor either distrusted his own abilities, or had not time to get up his case, for a recent discovery has shown that he unblushingly borrowed the whole of his defence from an earlier *Apologia*. Among the treasures of early patristic literature which have been discovered of recent years at the Monastery of Mount Sinai is a Syriac version of the *Apology of Aristides*. This was a second century treatise in defence of the faith, supposed to be addressed to the Emperor Hadrian. Eusebius appears to be the last person who had seen it, and it was supposed to have been irrevocably lost when Professor Rendell Harris printed and translated the Syriac version of it, which he had discovered on Mount Sinai. His friend, Prof. J. Armitage Robinson,* recollected that he had seen something very like it in *Barlaam and Josaphat*, and on comparing the two it was clear that the Greek Barlaam preserved a very large proportion of the original text.

This remarkable discovery naturally set theologians on the search for other traces of early Christian literature in the *Barlaam*, and sure enough, in another portion of the book, a sort of early Divine Comedy, Prof. Armitage Robinson discovered a direct "crib" from the Vision

---

* Prof. Robinson's discovery was made known in the first fascicule of the Cambridge *Texts and Studies*. A useful reconstruction of the text from the Greek and from the Syriac and Armenian versions has been recently produced by E. Hennecke as part of Gebhardt and Harnack's *Texte und Untersuchungen* (iv. 3, 1893).

of Saturus in the *Passio S. Perpetuæ*,* while other portions seem to show acquaintance with the still more recently discovered *Apocalypse of Peter*. Finally, it has been also observed that parts of the Greek Barlaam are derived from the *Scheda Regia* of Agapetus, finished in July 527. As there are no traces of the continued existence of the earlier works later than the sixth century, and as Agapetus' work had not much vogue for more than the few years after its appearance, it is clear that we can fix the date of the Greek Barlaam within a few years ± 600 A.D.†

* This forms the second fascicule of the *Texts and Studies*.

† Mr. F. C. Conybeare informs me that he is inclined to date the Greek text later, owing to references occurring in it to the Iconoclastic controversy.

II

THE ORIENTAL VERSIONS

IN arriving at some result as to the date of the Greek text we have certainly got to a station on the line of tradition which, as we shall see later, branches off in all directions right throughout Europe. But it remains to be seen whether this station is a terminus, a starting-point from which the train of tradition leaves with more or less of punctuality, or merely a junction towards which many of the branch lines converge. Even if we decided that the Greek text was a *terminus a quo* with regard to written tradition, we might have still to investigate whether its contents had not been brought to the Greek-speaking world by the mouths of men, and there transferred from the pack saddles of oral tradition to the broad gauge of literature.

The first of these questions to be settled is

clearly whether the *Barlaam* exists in an earlier literary form than the Greek text. At first sight Prof. Robinson's discoveries would seem to settle that question in a most decisive way. If the Greek text contains, as integral portions, slices of earlier Greek, it is almost impossible that these could have been introduced in the text except in a Greek form. And indeed, if the quotations from the *Apology of Aristides* and other early Christian texts were essential portions of the romance, the originality of its Greek form would be established beyond question. But these are clearly excrescences which could be removed or replaced without much derangement of the main plan, and we must look about to see if any versions exist which do not contain them.

Several such versions have been discovered in quite recent years. An Arabic one, running to no less than 286 pages, was printed in Bombay under the title *Kitâb Balauhar wa-Bûdâsaph* in 1889, while Dr. Hommel printed another Arabic version at the Vienna Oriental Congress.* Again, Dr. Steinschneider many

* Hommel's version was translated by Mr. E. Rehatsek in the Journal of the Roy. Asiat. Soc., xxii. 119-55. A

years ago discovered that one of the best known didactic poems in Mediæval Jewish literature, *The Prince and the Dervish*, by Abraham ibn Chisdai, was undoubtedly a version of the Barlaam legend. Lastly, a Mr. Marr has discovered and (partly) published a Georgian version of the legend under the title *Mudrost' Balavara*, or, "The Wisdom of Balavar." Almost any of these versions might be, or represent, the original form of the legend, and the present stage of Barlaam criticism is concerned with their relative antiquity and independence. Among these high summits of Oriental scholarship it is customary to tie oneself to the latest German * in order to avoid falling into the many crevasses in the path. In accordance with this custom I attach myself to Dr. Kuhn.

The most startling suggestion that has been made with regard to these recent discoveries of Oriental versions has been, that the Greek text was a translation from the Georgian. Baron von Rosen, in a review of M. Zoten-

third Arabic text has been interpolated into a theological work by Muhamad ibn Babawaik (ob. 991 A.D.). See Hommel ap. Weisslovits.

* But what if the latest German himself tumbles?

berg's book, brought forward a couple of pieces of evidence which at first sight seemed conclusive, coming as they do from such different sources, where there could be no question of collusion. Two of the MSS. of the Greek text (Nanianus 137, Paris, 1771) attributed the translation into Greek to a St. Euthymius. Now in a Grusinian life of St. Euthymius it is stated of him that he had translated *Balavari* and *Abukura*, and some other books from Georgian into Greek. Taking these two statements into connection with the fact that an ancient Georgian version of the Barlaam legend has been published by Marr, in which Barlaam goes by the name of Balavar, the conclusion seems almost forced upon us that this is the legend from which the Greek had been translated by Euthymius.

But further research and reflection prove that this conclusion is precipitate, even though Baron von Rosen and Professor Hommel have adopted it. The two Greek codices come from Mount Athos, where the tradition about St. Euthymius may be merely a bit of chauvinistic bluster, and is, at any rate, 400 years later than the composition of the Greek text.

Finally, the Georgian text differs widely from the Greek, and cannot therefore have been its original: while the unique MS. that contains it attributes it to "Sophron of Palestine, the son of Isaac." Things are not always what they seem when scholarly hypotheses are about.

Dismissing thus the Grusinian version out of the purview, there remain the various Arabic versions, and the Hebrew one, to assist us in our search after the *Urquelle*. And first with regard to the Arabic versions: considerable light is thrown by various references made in the *Kitâb al-Fihrist*, a sort of Arabic Lowndes or Brunet. This contains references in various places to no less than four books that may possibly have influenced the Barlaam literature. (*a*) A Buddha book, *Kitâb al-Budd*. (*b*) A *Kitâb Yudâsâf wa-Balauhar*. (*c*) A book of "Yudasaf alone" and (*d*) a poem of Aban ibn Abdal-Hamid (ob. 822), with the same title as (*b*). Excluding the last, which is no longer in existence, and can only have been of secondary importance, it seems clear that there existed a double set of books in Arabic, one dealing directly with Buddha and his legend, the other placing Balauhar by his side.

Leaving for a moment the book of Buddha, of which I fancy I have found traces, one has to settle the question of the relationship of the Georgian, Greek, and Arabic versions. From Appendix I., in which their variations are noted, it will be observed that the Georgian agrees with the Arabic version with regard to the original order of the parables: while, on the other hand, it agrees in omitting certain portions with the Greek, and in the conclusion of the story. Kuhn, accordingly, represents the relationship by the following genealogical tree :—

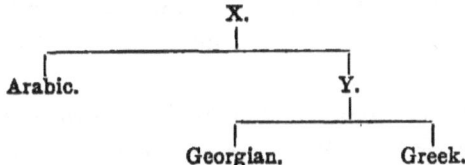

I have small Arabic and less Georgian, and I must therefore tread warily on this aspect of the question. But there seems to be one conclusive piece of evidence against the pedigree suggested by Dr. Kuhn. There can be no doubt what the unknown quantity Y is, as regards the Greek version. Syriac was the main conduit pipe through which the treasures of Greek literature debouched on to the Orient, and inversely, it was mainly through Syriac versions that Oriental treasures were added to Greco-Byzantine literature: and we have special reason for saying, as we shall soon see, that Syriac was the immediate source of the Greek version. But that the Georgian also derived from that language, as Dr. Kuhn suggests, the only external confirmation of the suggestion he can give, is its alleged authorship by Sophron of Palestine. Against it, and as I think, obviously against it, is the title of the Georgian version, which connects it with an Arabic, and disconnects it from a Syrian source.

Proper names are the *feu follet* of the etymologist, but the Pole Star of the literary historian; the one has to guess at their inner meaning, the other can follow the changes in their outer form. There can be no doubt how and why the name Barlaam got into the Greek version, instead of the form Balauhar, found in the recently discovered Oriental ones. Barlaam was an Antioch worthy of the early fourth century, who is referred to by SS. Basil and Chrysostom in their homilies; a church was erected to his honour in Edessa, 411 A.D.* Outside Syria he was unknown, and his name must have been introduced in the Syriac version from its accidental similarity with the Balauhar of the Arabic version. Now, if the Georgian had been derived from the Syriac, it would surely have retained the form, Barlaam, instead of keeping, as it has, to the Arabic form, Balauhar. Considering, too, that the order of the parables are the same in the Georgian and Arabic versions, I think there can be little doubt that it was derived from the Arabic, and the variations at the end may have been due to later modifications of the Bombay Arabic text, intended to modify its Christianising tendencies.

There is still another form in which the Buddha legend got into Syriac. Professor Hommel has already suggested that the earlier part of the legend of St. Alexis, in which that saint flees from wife and child in order to embrace the

* Hommel gives these details in Weisslovits, 141.

hermit's life, is simply a Christian adaptation of the Great Renunciation of Siddartha the Buddha. The late M. Amiaud, who studied the Greek forms of the legend, *La Légende Syriaque de S. Alexis*, Paris, 1889, came to the conclusion that it was written c. 450–75, originally without any name being attached to it, and without the second part, dealing with an impossible journey to "Rome," probably Constantinople. Curiously enough, in this early version the anonymous "holy man" is represented to have died at Edessa, 412, the very date within a year when the Church was dedicated to St. Barlaam. As this early life is solely devoted to the Great Renunciation, and was originally anonymous, I venture to suggest that it was derived directly or indirectly from the original of the Buddha book (*Kitâb al-Budd*), mentioned in the *Fihrist*. Whether the relation of the Alexis legend to the Church of St. Barlaam was accidental or not, it is indeed curious that the name of this otherwise unknown saint has become connected with both the Syriac forms of the Buddha legend.

Reverting to these given above, we have still

to determine the unknown quantity X in Kuhn's pedigree. Here we are helped by the other name in our title. Yudasaph is frequently referred to elsewhere in Arabic literature as the founder of an Indian ascetic religion. The same name is found written Budasaph, with merely the change of a diacritical point. Reinaud was the first to suggest that the latter variant was simply a form of Bodhisattva, the technical term in Buddhistic literature for the man who is destined to become a Buddha. But where and how did Bodhisattva become Bodasaph? Obviously in Persia, where the ending *asp* is a favourite one for proper names.

Another name confirms this result in a most instructive way. When the young prince, in the story, goes out for the first time into the world and sees some of its misery, he is accompanied by his teacher, whose name is Zardan in the Greek, Zandani in the Georgian version. There is little doubt that these forms are ultimately to be derived from Chandaka, the Buddha's charioteer. The variation of the Greek and Georgian forms can only be explained by their derivation from a script in which *n* and *r* are indistinguishable. This occurs in the Pehlevi alphabet, and not in the Syriac: so I am again confirmed in my dissent from Dr. Kuhn's* view, that the Georgian was derived from the Syriac version. The Georgian form, Zandani, is at least a step closer to India. Incidentally the name tells us from what part of India the legend was derived. Among the Buddhists of Southern India the Master's charioteer is known as Channa, among those of the North he has the fuller name, Chandaka. By the presence of the *d* in the Georgian and Greek forms we learn that their source is to be found, as was to be expected, among the Northern Buddhists.

We still have to determine the relations of the

---

* The sentence in which Dr. Kuhn states the above facts, with the requisite references, fills seventeen lines of his Memoir, pp. 34-5, and includes no less than 230 words. It is in other respects a model German scientific sentence, and I would have quoted it as a warning example, but that I owe so much to Dr. Kuhn, and feel that its clumsiness is not personal to him, but merely characteristic of the want of consideration for their readers shown by German scientific writers.

three various Arabic texts which are still extant, with that of the Hebrew version of Abraham ibn Chisdai (ob. 1240). The difficulty here is put at once by the opening words of ibn Chisdai's version : " Thus saith the translator from the Greek into Arabic." Besides the rarity of such direct translations, without the intermediation of Syriac, there is the further difficulty that the Hebrew version does not entirely agree, either in order or in contents, with any of the Arabic texts at present accessible. It comes nearer to the Halle MS., but that on the face of it is only an extract. Professor Hommel, and his pupil, Dr. Weisslovits, claim for the Hebrew version a closer relationship with the Pehlevi original than is the case with the Greek : and though Dr. Kuhn seems opposed to the claim, it would seem to be confirmed by the agreement of the Hebrew with the order of the parables in the Arabic texts, which again agrees with that of the Georgian to which we have assigned a closer relationship to the Pehlevi version.

The following table of Professor Hommel will indicate this :—

Parable.	Georgian.	Hebrew.	Arabic. (Halle and Razi.)	Greek.
Death Trumpet	1	c. viii.	1	2
The Four Caskets	2	c. viii.	2	3
The Sower	3	c. x.	3	1
Man in Well	4	...	4	5
The Three Friends	5	c. xi.	5	6
King of the Year	6	c. xiii.	6	7
King and Vizier	7	c. xvi.	7	8
Rich Man and Beggar's Daughter	8	c. xviii.	8*	9
Man and Nightingale	9	c. xxi.	9	4
The Tame Gazelle	10	...	...	10
The Amorous Wife	11†	...	...	...
The Demon Women	12	...	...	11

The order of the parables is here the same in the Hebrew, Arabic, and Georgian, while that of the Greek varies considerably. The absence of the last three parables in Hebrew and Arabic is simply due to the fact that they do not contain anything subsequent to the parting with Barlaam. But the variation of order in the Greek text against the unanimity of the other three versions seems to me conclusive against the mediate derivation of the Hebrew or Arabic from the Greek, which may there-

* Wanting in the Halle MS.
† This occurs only in the Georgian version, but has analogies with similar tales in the *Katha Sarit Sagara*, in which the lustful disposition of woman is insisted upon.

fore for the present be set aside in our journey to the *fons et origo* of the whole literature.

Thus far we are led to the conclusion that this original was in Pehlevi, and on this point there is, practically, unanimity among recent investigators. But the book, on the face of it, is propagandist, and the question arises, what religion was it whose interests it was composed to further? Dr. Kuhn declares for a Christian author, but on very slight grounds, as it seems to me. True, there is a certain amount of evidence for the existence of a Christian Pehlevi literature.* True, the Nestorian Church was firmly established in East Iran. The possibility, therefore, of the Christian manipulation of the Buddha legend in that district cannot be denied. But the Barlaam book in its Pehlevi form had very little theological tendency. The theologisms of the Greek text are excrescences, and are peculiar to that version. The only trace of Christian influence to which Dr. Kuhn can point, is the parable of *The Sower*, to which, curiously enough, there are strong Buddhistic parallels (Carus, *Gospel*

* Professor Sachau in Journal Roy. Asiat. Soc. N.S., iv. 230, *seq*.

of Buddha. I cannot think that any work, written with the express view of the propagation of the faith, would be so singularly free from all dogmatic colouring.

The existence of the Hebrew version confirms me in my belief that the original work was not intended, or regarded, as specifically religious, or, at any rate, theological. Its teaching is ascetic, it is true, but all religions have a touch of asceticism. It was for the sake of its parables, not for its theology, that the book was taken up, equally by Moslem, Jewish, and Christian writers. Now the Hebrew version is much fuller in its parables, containing no less than ten * not found in the other versions. Of these, four at least can be traced back to India (*Bird and Angel*, *The Power of Love*, *Language of Animals*, and *Robbers' Nemesis*). I see no reason, therefore, why we should not go behind the Pehlevi and look for the original in its complete form, as we can certainly trace it in its elements, to India itself.

* *Bird and Angel*, c. ix.; *Cannibal King*, c. xii.; *The Good Physician*, c. xiv.; *King and Pious Shepherd;* *Oasis and Garden*, c. xvi.; *The Hungry Bitch*, c. xvii.; *The Power of Love*, c. xviii.; *Eel and Dog*, c. xxiii.; *The Language of Animals*, c. xxiv.; *The Robbers' Nemesis*.

In short, I regard the literary history of the Barlaam literature as completely parallel with that of the Fables of Bidpai. Originally Buddhistic books, both lost their specifically Buddhistic traits before they left India, and made their appeal, by their parables, more than by their doctrines. Both were translated into Pehlevi in the reign of Chosroes, and from that watershed floated off into the literatures of all the great creeds. In Christianity alone, characteristically enough, one of them, the Barlaam book, was surcharged with dogma and turned to polemical uses, with the curious result that Buddha became one of the champions of the Church. To divest the Barlaam-Buddha of this character, and see him in his original form, we must take a further journey and seek him in his home beyond the Himalayas.

III.

Barlaam in India.

The Portuguese historian, Diogo do Conto, in describing the exploits of his nation in Asia, in 1612, had occasion to speak of Buddha, or the Budão, as he called him. After recounting his legend, he goes on to say: "With reference to this story, we have been delayed in inquiring if the ancient Gentiles of those parts had in their writings any knowledge of Josaphat, who was converted by Barlaam, who in his legend is represented as the son of a great king in India, who had just the same up-bringing, with all the same particulars that we have recounted of the life of the Budão . . . and as it informs us that he was the son of a great king in India, it may well be, as we have said, that *he* was the Budão of whom they relate such marvels"* (*Decada*

---

* The late Sir Henry Yule drew attention to this remarkable anticipation of modern research in the *Academy* *quinta da Asia*, l. vi. c. ii., Lisboa, 1612, f. 123).

Thus, almost as soon as the Western world got to know anything of the Buddha, the remarkable resemblance of his legend and that of St. Josaphat was observed, but no note was taken of do Conto's hint for two centuries and a half, when M. Laboulaye, quite independently, drew attention to the Buddhistic origin of the Barlaam legend in the *Journal des Debats* of the 26th July 1859.* Laboulaye's discovery was clinched by Felix Liebrecht in a paper on the sources of Barlaam and Josaphat (Jahrbuch, f. Rom. Lit. 1860, 314-34).† Since the appearance of that striking memoir, no doubt has ever existed in any one's mind, who has examined the question of the legend of St. Joasaph, that it was simply and solely derived from the legend of Buddha. Indeed, if we put the two legends side by side, as M. Cosquin has done (*Contes de Lorraine*, pp. xlix. *seq.*), their close resemblance, if not identity, is

of 1st Sept. 1883. He repeats the information in his *Marco Polo*, ii. 308.

* Dr. Steinschneider had suspected the Indian origin nine years before in ZDMG, v. 91.

† Reprinted in his *Zur Volkskunde*, 1879, pp. 441-60.

"proved by inspection," as the mathematicians say.

JOASAPH.	BUDDHA.
Abenner, King of India, persecutes the Christians. He has a beautiful son, named Joasaph. An Astrologer reveals to the King that he will become a Christian.	Suddhodana, King of Kapilavastu, in India, has a beautiful son, who is called Siddharta. The Brahmins predict that he will become a Hermit.
The King builds a magnificent palace in a remote district, in which he places his son, and surrounds him by those who are ordered never to speak of the miseries of this life, of sickness, poverty, old age, or death.	The King builds three palaces for his son—one for the Spring, one for the Summer, and one for the Winter. Each palace is surrounded by five hundred Guards. The Prince desires one day to visit their garden. The King orders everything to be removed that could indicate the existence of misery.
When Joasaph is grown up he asks permission to go outside the palace. On his way he sees a leper and a blind man. He asks what is the cause of their appearance. He is told that it is due to illnesses caused by the corruption of the humours, and learns that every man is liable to similar evils. He becomes sad and distressed.	Going out of the South Gate of his palace the Prince sees on the footpath a sick man burning with fever, breathing heavily, and emaciated. Learning from his charioteer the cause of this, the Prince exclaims, "How can man think of joy and pleasure when such things exist!" and turning back his chariot he re-enters the palace.
Shortly afterwards, Joa-	Another day, going out

JOASAPH.	BUDDHA.
saph on another excursion comes across an old man, bent double, with tottering steps, white hair, wrinkled visage, and toothless gums. He asks his attendants what this means. They tell him it is due to old age. "And what will be the end of it all?" he asks. "No other than death," they reply. "And is that the end of all men?" asks the Prince, and learns that sooner or later death comes to all men. From that day the Prince is plunged in thinking to himself, "One day death will carry me off too; shall I be swallowed up into nothing? Or is there another life, or another world?"	of the East Gate, he comes across an old man, decrepit, wrinkled, bent, and tottering, with white hairs. "Who is this man?" he asks. "And why does he look so strange? Is he of some peculiar species of men? Or do all men become like that?" His charioteer replies, "This man's appearance is due to his age, and all men become like him when they are old." The Prince orders his charioteer to turn back, saying, "If such an old age awaits me, what have I to do with pleasure and joy?"
	Going out another time by the West Gate, he sees a dead man on a bier, his relatives mourning round him. He learns what death is, and cries out, "Wretched youth, that old age can destroy! Wretched health, that so many maladies can destroy! Wretched life where man remains for so short a time!"
The Hermit Barlaam ap-	The fourth time the Prince

JOASAPH.	BUDDHA.
pears under disguise to Joasaph, tells him of Christianity, and converts him. After the departure of Barlaam, Joasaph tries to lead the life of a Hermit in his palace.	goes out by the North Gate, when he sees a Bhikshu, calm and reserved, with cast-down eyes, carrying an alms-dish. He asks what sort of man this is, and is told that he is an Ascetic, who has renounced all passion and ambition, and lives on charity. "It is well," says Siddharta; "I have found the clue to the miseries of life." And once more he returns to the palace.
The King tries every means to turn Joasaph from the true faith, but in vain.	The Prince informs his father of his intention to become an Ascetic. The King tries to dissuade him, but in vain.

After this exercise on the parallel bars there can be no doubt of the identity of Josaphat and Buddha. As we have already seen, their very names are the same, for Josaphat is only the Roman spelling for Yosaphat, this again being a confusion between the Biblical Jehoshaphat and the Greek form Joasaph. This is directly derived from the Arabic; it is a contracted form of Yodasaph,* which is a mis-

* Kuhn explains it is as a misspelling, ΙΩΑΑΣΑΦ for ΙΩΔΑΣΑΦ.

reading for Bodasaph, since *y* and *b* in Arabic are only distinguished by a diacritical point. As we have already seen, Bodasaph is directly derived, through the Pehlevi, from *Bodhisattva*, the technical title of the man who is destined to attain Buddhahood, a description that exactly applies to the career of Josaphat. The very name, therefore, of the hero implies a conscious Buddhistic tendency in the original form of the legend, and tells against Dr. Kuhn's contention for a Pehlevi Christian original.

It is also probable that the first name in our title can also be traced back to India, but on the exact form, which was the original, learned opinion is not at present united: and a mere reporter, like myself, can only put the conflicting claims before the reader and allow him to take his choice. We have seen that Barlaam is merely a Syriac substitute for Balauvar. Dr. Kuhn points out, that in the Zend alphabet *g* and *l* are almost identical, while we have already seen that *n* and *r* might easily mistake themselves for one another. Consequently, this pundit suggests * *Bhagavan* is the real original

---

* When I was at Cambridge, the boat of the Non-Collegiate students was generally known as the *Non Coll.*

of *balauhar*. Unfortunately, he leaves us in the dark as to what *Bhagavan* means or implies. It is, of course, one of the titles given to the Buddha. Baron von Rosen, on the other hand, identifies *Balauhar* with an Arabic word, *balahvar*, used by the Arabic lexicographers to designate an Indian king. The reader will not be surprised to learn that the Arabic word is a simple adaptation of the Sanskrit *bhattaraka*. Both suggestions seem to me almost equally far-fetched. But the human-mind is incapable of remaining in a state of suspension *à la* Buridan. De Morgan said that he found most people had a decided view on the question whether platythliptic coefficients were positive or negative.* Similarly, if one has to make a choice, Dr. Kuhn's

---

Boat. One day it suddenly made its appearance as the *Heron.* The whole University was puzzled at the change, till a budding philologist remarked casually, "Of course, they are the same. 'Non Coll.' becomes by transposition 'Coll-on,' and this by metathesis of *l* and *r* becomes 'coron.' Aspiration of the initial consonant changes it to 'choron,' which, again, by weakening of the aspirate and vernerising the vowel, becomes 'Heron.' Thus 'Non-Coll' = 'Heron.' Q.E.D."

* We are getting more modest nowadays. I have fired off this query at most of my friends, who persist in spoiling De Morgan's point by asking, "What are platythliptic coefficients ?"

suggestion seems to have more for it than Baron von Rosen's. For there is little doubt that, as a matter of fact, Barlaam is himself a variant of the Buddha, and thus a doublet of Josaphat. For Barlaam's speeches give very often the Buddhistic doctrine in the Buddha's own words: so that, in the last resort, our fable tells of the conversion of the man destined to be Buddha by a man who has already attained Buddhahood, and the title, "Barlaam and Josaphat," would adequately indicate the subject to Indian ears in the form *Bhagavan Bodhisattvascha.** We get the same doubling in the Buddha legend when the Buddha converts to his doctrines a rich merchant's son named Yasoda,† who has himself performed the Great Renunciation, and whose history is therefore obviously a variant of the Buddha's.

We have seen that other names still retain traces of their Indian origin. Josaphat's tutor,

* I have to thank my young friend, Master Leonard Magnus, for my knowledge how to conjoin two Sanskrit words. If there is anything incorrect, I must have misunderstood his instructions. I would add that Marco Polo's title for the Buddha "Sagamoni Borcar"=Sakyamuni Bhagavan.

† Vesselovsky would identify the name Joasaph with this Yasoda.

Zardan, was, we saw, Buddha's charioteer, Chandaka. Kuhn gives several other examples, chiefly, however, derived from the Arabic version: for the Greek has, in most instances, substituted Biblical, or quasi-Biblical, names for the original. Thus, Josaphat's father, in the Arabic, Janaisar, becomes in the Greek, Abenner (2 Sam. iii. 6). The Rakis of the Arabic appears in double form in the Greek, as Araches and Nachor, the latter being derived from Genesis xi. Similarly, the magician Theudas is derived from Acts v. 37, and has only an accidental resemblance to Devadatta, the Judas of the Buddha legend. But, besides these merely formal proofs of Indian origin derived from the names, there is much internal evidence for the influence of Indian thought. Even the Greek text preserves traces of Buddhistic phraseology, as Dr. Berry has shown. Thus, in the earlier part of the book, where one of the king's nobles takes to the hermit's life, it is said of him "that with noble purpose he purified his senses by fasting and watching, and by the diligent study of sacred articles. And having delivered his soul from every kind of emotion he shone with the light of dispassionate calm." Again, at the end of the book, when Abenner becomes converted, a great multitude of his people are baptized, "both rulers and civil officers, soldiers and people," a distinct reference to the four castes of India.

But it is especially in the recently printed Bombay text of the Arabic version that we find the clearest and most conclusive proof of the complete identification of Josaphat and Barlaam in the original. Here we find, not alone the Great Renunciation, in which Josaphat, like Buddha, leaves power, wealth, love, and family ties behind him at the dead of night, but even the meditation under the Bo-Tree.* In this version, indeed, the Buddha and his doctrines are especially referred to by name, as "al-Budd," and the dying Budasaph, like the dying Buddha, breathes his last in the arms of his favourite disciple Anand. Dr. Kuhn suggests that these details and references are due to interpolations by the Arabic translators from some of the lost Arabic books relating to Buddha, mentioned in the *Fihrist*. But this is all conjecture, and is mainly urged by Dr.

* See Abstract of Legend in App. I. xiii.

Kuhn to support his contention that the original of Barlaam literature was a Pehlevi Christian adaptation of Christian legends. For my part, I cannot see any evidence for any distinctive dogmatic colouring in the original. As is shown by a comparison with the Georgian, the distinctively Christian passages of the Greek version are interpolations peculiar to it (see App. I. vi., viii., ix., xiii.), or at least to its immediate Syriac source. Removing these interpolations, the original is seen to be entirely and characteristically Buddhistic in form and contents, and we cannot imagine such a work originating elsewhere than in India.

On the other hand, it seems likely that none of the Arabic versions represent completely the original Indian source of them all. They omit the veneration of Josaphat's relics, which is a distinct Buddhistic touch, as Liebrecht saw (*Zur Volkskunde*, 454–5).* The detrition to which the proper names have been subjected in the Arabic text show a long course of transmission, and we cannot, therefore, depend

---

* Kuhn is therefore mistaken (p. 32) in thinking this an independent interpolation of the common source of the Georgian and Greek version.

implicitly upon it for even an approximate restoration of the Indian original. Yet sufficient remains of this for us to be enabled to come to a tolerably definite conclusion as to the early history of the Barlaam legend before it took its Greek form. That history may be shortly summarised as follows.

During the declining years of Buddhism in India, in the early centuries of our era, attempts were made by the Brahmins to adopt that side of the Buddhistic methods which had proved most attractive, namely, the method of teaching by parables. A number of the most striking of these were adopted by the Brahmins and placed in a beast-tale framework, and formed the Indian original of the Fables of Bidpai. In opposition to this, the Buddhists retold the legend of the Buddha in a form least adapted to arouse Brahmanistic opposition, but equally enriched with the most striking of Buddhistic parables. It recounted the attaining the Buddhahood by a Bodhisattva, or one destined to be a Buddha, owing to the teachings of a Bhagavan, or one who has already attained the Supreme State. This latter book received some such title as *Bhagavan Bodhisattvascha*, and was the original of our *Barlaam*. Both of these Buddhistic books were translated into Pehlevi in the reign of Chosroes (531–79 A.D.), and both proved attractive to all the various sects—Buddhistic, Moslem, Nestorian—that found a common point of contact in East Iran. Both were almost immediately translated into Arabic and Syriac, and passed from the latter into almost all the languages of Europe. But the beast-tales of Bidpai were incapable of any dogmatic colouring, and were left unchanged in the European versions. The story of the conversion of the Bodhisattva by the Bhagavan was, on the other hand, admirably adapted for propagandist interpolation and modification, and was therefore transformed by the Greek translator into the legend of St. Barlaam and St. Josaphat, as it afterwards spread through Europe. It was thus the difference of the framework which led to a difference in fate between the Bidpai and the Barlaam legends. But in both cases the attractiveness of the books consisted, not so much in the framework, as in that which it enframed, to which we now turn.

IV.

Parables of Barlaam

For some reason or other, which has never yet been fully investigated, there is nothing so irritating to humanity, nothing so boring, as the inculcation to morality. Whether it is that we feel instinctively that we know what is right even if we do not do it, and therefore need not be told it, or whether we resent being told by another, who thereby lays claim to greater moral insight than ourselves, the result is certain, nothing makes people feel so wicked as moral exhortations. Nowadays the moralists know this; formerly they only suspected it. So in former days they invented the Parable so as to administer the moral pill in the story jam.

Greece and India, I have shown elsewhere, each invented separately the Fable as a means of moral or political instruction.* Similarly Judea and India, each probably independently, invented the Parable for the same purpose. Both the Rabbis and the Brahmins found that the best way to point a moral was to adorn a tale. Both Jesus and Buddha adopted the method of their rivals for the purpose of their propaganda.† Especially was this the case with Buddha and his followers. A very large part of the Buddhist Scriptures is taken up by parables, and it is to this source that we can ultimately trace the parables of Barlaam, which, equally with those of Bidpai, may be described as the Parables of Buddha.

And, first, what is a Parable? It is a tale with a double meaning, like the Fable or the Allegory. It is distinguished from the Fable as being told of men, not beasts; from the Allegory, by its shortness and greater directness. The Sunday School definition, "An earthly story with a heavenly meaning," is too

---

* See Caxton, Æsop, i. p. 209.

† It is characteristic that in his special treatise on the Parables Archbishop Trench treated those of the Rabbis most perfunctorily, though there can be no doubt Jesus learnt the method from them.

restricted, since many parables know nothing of heaven or hell. The Parable is often merely an Example of a moral truth which it is intended to convey, but it should more strictly be defined as a Narrative-Metaphor. As with the Metaphor, the Parable often leads to false reasoning when the analogy is pushed too far.

Whatever their origin, use, or effectiveness, there is no doubt of their popularity among all creeds in the Middle Ages. Brahmins, Rabbis, Monks, and Moolahs all enliven their religious discussions with a seasoning of parables. The illicit joys of tale and gossip were used to evade the *longueurs* of the sermon. In Christendom the fashion chimed in with the vogue for the allegorical interpretation of Scripture, by which its insufficiency was eked out or its inconsistencies overcome. And the fashion spread from the moral sermon to the moral treatise till there was scarcely a mediæval book of devotion which did not relieve its preternatural dulness by some form or other of the parable. Perhaps the most favourite source for these *divertissements* was the Legend of Barlaam and Josaphat, which, in a way, forms the centre of the whole literature. Its parables, therefore, form a type of a whole literary movement in Europe and Asia, and to them we may now turn.

Taking all the earliest versions of the Barlaam Legend, the Arabic, Georgian, Hebrew, and Greek, there appear to be some three dozen parables contained in them. But, as is the case with more important gospels, those of Barlaam are not entirely synoptic. Some of the parables appear in all forms, and of these we may be sure all could be traced back to India. Others again appear but in two or three of these versions, while a considerable number only make their appearance in one version, *e.g.*, the Hebrew or the Bombay Arabic. I have told them all in Appendix II., and given the details of their occurrences in the earliest versions of *Barlaam*, as well as the history of their spread outside the specifically Barlaam literature. Here I propose treating of them more generally in the first place, and then descanting at greater length on a few of the parables which happen to be of exceptional interest from their widespread or their important derivates.

Of the thirty-one parables contained in Appendix II., nine occur in all the earlier versions, six occur in two or more of them, while sixteen have found their way to only one version. Of the first class, six can be traced to India; of the second, two; and of the third, seven. It does not, therefore, appear that any very certain proof of existence in the original *Barlaam* is shown by the absence or presence of traceable Indian parallels. Indeed, no mechanical and external test can enable us to judge whether any special parable came with *Barlaam* from India. Even where, as in some of the parables, especially to the Hebrew version, an Indian original has been found, it by no means follows that the parable in question, though ultimately derived from India, necessarily came into the Hebrew version from some form of the Barlaam Legend. Thus it would be premature to assume, *e.g.*, that the story known as *The Language of Animals* first began its travels through the ages and the climes in connection with the Legend of Barlaam-Buddha. The spread of these parables, extensive as it is, throws but little light on the diffusion of folktales properly so called. In almost every case the spread has been by means of literary, not oral, tradition. Those that occur in the Greek version were translated into Latin, and were then utilised as *Exempla*, or seasoning for sermons. And it was from this source, if at all, that they became current among the folk. In the discussion about the diffusion of popular literature the question of Indian origin has to be treated separately, according to the character of the tales involved. These may be divided into four classes: fables, parables, stories of the wiles of women, and folktales. As far as the evidence goes at present, it would seem that the first two classes were transmitted by literary colportage, while the second two have passed from East to West, from mouth to mouth.*

Of the wide spread which many of these parables of Barlaam reached, ample evidence is given in Appendix II. Though the references there are put in the shortest and, I fear, most

---

* Hence it is that M. Bédier, in his ingenious work on the *Fabliaux*, which seem to be mainly derived from the third class, is entirely beating the air in attempting to disprove their derivation from Indian *books*. M. Gaston Paris had put M. Bédier's whole argument out of court when he stated of the *Fabliaux*, "Ils proviennent de la transmission orale et non des livres" (*Lit. franç.*, § 73).

unintelligible form, and in the smallest of legible type, in several cases they take up a whole page, without any claim to be exhaustive. It would, obviously, be impossible to discuss here all, or even a majority, of these parables, ample information about which can be obtained in the critical treatment of them, for which I give references in Appendix II. under the section of "Literature." But it seems desirable to treat at greater length a few of the more important parables, whether their importance depends upon their illustrious derivates or their folklore interest. Of these there can be no doubt which comes first in every way in deserving special notice.

1. *The Four Caskets.*—To find an integral part of the plot of one of Shakspere's best-known plays to be derived from Indian parable is one of those curiosities of literature which cannot fail to strike even the most vacant mind. But that the Caskets Story of the *Merchant of Venice* can ultimately be derived from a Buddhistic legend there is no manner of doubt, even if the immediate source whence Shakspere drew it cannot at present be ascertained. We can at least trace the

story from India to England through the medium of the Barlaam literature, and there can be no doubt that it came to Shakspere through some derivate of the *Gesta Romanorum*, the English end link in the chain of tradition. But even apart from this evidence, the internal proofs of relationship would be decisive.

A reference to the form of the Parable as it appears in the Barlaam Literature (see Appendix II., *infra*, p. cvii.) will convince the reader that he has there the original Shaksperian *motif*. It is there found combined with the Parable of *The Trumpet of Death* in such a way as to make up one complex story. Now there can be no doubt about the Buddhistic origin of the Parable of *The Trumpet of Death*. It is found separately told of Vityasoka, brother of the great Buddhistic King, Asoka. The great King's brother, who had not yet been converted to Buddhism, had expressed his wonder that the followers of that religion could overcome their passions without resorting to asceticism. The King, to try his brother, and to convert him to the New Religion—so runs the tale—ordered his courtiers to induce his brother and heir to try on the Royal Robes and sit upon the throne while he himself was at the Bath. The King, however, managed to catch his brother in his compromising attitude on the throne, and ordered him as a punishment to be treated as a King for a week, except that behind the throne was placed all the time the Royal Executioner with his Warning Bell. After the week was over the King asked his brother how he had managed so well to overcome his passions without resorting to asceticism. Vityasoka replied that he could think of nothing but the impending death with which the Executioner kept threatening him. "If you could be so influenced by the thought of one death," said the King, "how much more we Buddhists, who have to think of an innumerable series of deaths through all the phases of our existence." The brother was convinced, and joined the new Creed. (Burnouf, *Introduction à l'Histoire de Buddhisme:* Paris, 1876, p. 370.)

That this is the original of the Barlaam Parable no one will deny; whether it is itself derived from an earlier Indian original of the

Story of Damocles, is another and more difficult question.

Curiously enough, however, no Indian original has yet been discovered for the *Story of the Four Caskets*, which, in the *Barlaam*, is so closely connected with the *Trumpet of Death*. Dr. Braunholtz, who has made a most complete study of this parable,* has failed to find anything nearer than Buddhistic comparisons of man's body to a casket. There is, it is true, a choice of four vessels occurring in the legend of the Buddha.† When the Buddha had finished his week's meditation under the Bo-Tree, two merchants, who became his first two converts, approached him and offered him rice and honey in a golden vessel. He refused the refreshment on the ground of the costly nature of the vessel containing it, and continued to do so even after they had changed the vessel for a silver, and then for a copper one. Only when it was placed in the Clay Bowl, so famous in Buddhistic Legend, did he accept it.‡ This case of

---

* For title, *see* Append. II., *sub voce*, "Literature."
† Omitted from Carus, l. c. § xiii.
‡ Attempts have been made to trace the Holy Grail to this Almsdish; *see* Mr. Nutt's careful examination of the

choice is, however, only one of modesty, and has nothing to do with judgment by appearances, which is of the essence of the Caskets Story of Barlaam and Shakspere.

Dr. Braunholtz suggests that the idea of the choice may be derived from a widespread folktale, found throughout the Indo-European world, in which two girls go successively into Fairyland, and have there offered them a choice of caskets. The good girl chooses the least costly, and finds, on arriving home, that it is full of jewels. The other girl greedily selects the most expensive, and finds herself disappointed. This story has, indeed, the choice of caskets, but its moral is rather "Be modest" than "Do not judge by appearances," and thus resembles rather the choice of the Clay Bowl in the Legend of the Buddha than the selection of the Leaden Casket by Bassanio. It is, however, found in countries where Buddhism has had sway, as in Burmah and Japan, and is thus, possibly, of Buddhistic origin. But it can be only used on the present occasion to show that

---

suggestion in *Arch. Rev.*, iii 257-71, and my letter, *ibid.*, iv. 79, from which it would appear that the actual Dish still exists at Candahar.

a choice of caskets was a familiar *motif* in Buddhistic Legend, and thus make more probable the Buddhistic origin of the Casket Story.

But even without this confirmatory evidence the Buddhistic origin of the story can scarcely be doubted upon the evidence before us. It occurs in the Arabic and Georgian versions, as well as in the Greek, and was, therefore, in the Pehlevi and its Indian original. It is enframed in what is after all only a Life of Buddha, and is closely connected with the *Trumpet of Death*, the Buddhistic original of which has already been shown. One can have little hesitation in adding it to the store of Buddhistic parables, even though, up to the present, modern research has failed to discover it in Buddhistic literature. Of the former spread of the legend in the form in which it appears in the *Barlaam* Dr. Braunholtz gives full evidence. He has managed to put his elaborate researches in a pedigree, which I repeat in a modified form for the benefit of my readers. He combines with his inquiry a somewhat similar Folktale of *The Treasure in the Tree*, which develops into a story of two blind men, to one of whom a loaf of bread is given by the Emperor, in which some gold is hidden. This has only the faintest similarity with the Caskets Story, and I have, therefore, removed it and its derivates from the pedigree, which is thus entirely confined to the story we know so well from Shakspere.

2. *The Sower.*—The "Parable of the Sower," mostly as it is found in the Synoptic Gospels, occurs also in all the earliest versions of the *Barlaam*, Arabic, Georgian, Hebrew, and Greek. At first sight this fact does not seem to need much comment, but in reality it forms, perhaps, the chief puzzle in the critical problem of *Barlaam;* for it constitutes almost the only piece of definitely Christian origin in the *Ur-Barlaam*, as far as we can trace it. It is, therefore, the only piece of evidence for Dr. Kuhn's contention that *Barlaam* was originally written in Pehlevi by a Nestorian Christian for the polemical purposes of his faith. One might argue, in reply, that one parable does not make a theology, and that a Christian allegory might be used by a Buddhist somewhat in the way that Stanley or Jowett might use a rousing sentence of Mahomet or Buddha to point their Broad Church morals.

But there is a further point of interest and of difficulty about this parable in the present connection. Can we be quite sure that it is exclusively Christian? For there is also a Buddhistic "Parable of the Sower," which is given, as follows, in Dr. Carus' admirable *Gospel of Buddha* (§ lxxiv.):—

"Bhâradvâja, a wealthy Brahman, was celebrating his harvest thanksgiving when the Blessed One came with his alms-bowl, begging for food.

"Some of the people paid him reverence, but the Brahman was angry, and said, 'O Shramana, it would suit you better to go to work than to go begging. I plough and sow, and having ploughed and sown, I eat. If you did likewise, you too would have to eat.'

"And the Tathâgata answered him and said, 'O Brahman, I too plough and sow, and having ploughed and sown, I eat.'

"'Do you profess to be a husbandman?' replied the Brahman. 'Where, then, are your bullocks? Where is the seed and the plough?'

"The Blessed One said, 'Faith is the seed I sow; good works are the rain that fertilises it;

wisdom and modesty are the plough; my mind is the guiding rein; I lay hold of the handle of the law; earnestness is the goad I use; and exertion is my draught-ox. This ploughing is ploughed to destroy the weeds of illusion. The harvest it yields is the immortal life of Nirvâna, and thus all sorrow ends.'

"Then the Brahman poured rice-milk into a golden bowl and offered it to the Blessed One, saying, 'Let the teacher of mankind partake of the rice-milk, for the venerable Gautama ploughs a ploughing that bears the fruit of immortality.'"

Now at first sight this certainly seems a remarkable parallel to the Gospel parable, while its occasion is so natural that, if there is any question of derivation, the presumption is on the side of Buddha. But, examined more closely, the resemblance loses much of its force. For, while in the Buddhistic form stress is laid upon the sowing itself, in the Christian it is upon the nature of the soil to which attention is drawn. The moral of Buddha is—"Teaching is work;" the moral of Christ is—"The effect of teaching depends upon the character of the taught." Altogether, therefore, notwithstanding the striking resemblance, there is no need to discuss the possibilities of direct derivation.

But the resemblance is close enough to suggest that the Christian form of the parable was introduced instead of the Buddhistic one after "Barlaam" had left India; in other words, in the lost Pehlevi version.

3. *Man in Well.*—This parable, as will be seen from the references in App. II., was one of the most popular morals of mediæval sermonisers. Indeed, it puts in a most vivid form the most central practical doctrine of both Christian and Buddhistic Ethics. The supreme attraction of the pleasures of the senses amidst all the dangers of life and the perpetual threat of death has never been more vividly expressed. Of its specifically Indian character there can be no doubt. Dr. Kuhn, in an admirable monograph on the parable which he contributed to the complimentary volume presented to Professor von Böhtlingk on the Jubilee of his Doctor's degree (*Festgruss*, pp. 68-76), has given several instances outside the parable in which the *ficus indica religiosa* is made a symbol of life, notably in the *Bhagavad gita* (xv. i.),

where there is a tree whose branches are the elements and whose leaves are the things of sense coloured by good and ill. Again, there is the marvellous tree Ilpa, from whose branches honey or soma trickles (Benfey, *l. c.*, 83).

But we are not only dependent upon general analogies for the proof of the Indian origin of this parable. Benfey discovered two forms of the parable in the Chinese Buddhistic work entitled *Avadana*. Mr. Clouston * has found it in the eleventh book of the *Mahabharata*, and Dr. Kuhn has traced it in a Jaina work. Here we have the parable, not alone traced to India, but, in the Avadana and Jaina forms, closely connected with Buddhism. The story occurs in some of the Arabic forms of the Fables of Bidpai, whence it got into Europe through another source than the *Barlaam*. In the Bombay Arabic version of *Barlaam* there are distinctive peculiarities which are of critical importance, though this has not hitherto been observed. Most of these versions resemble one another, generally both in the story and in the allegory which it is intended to adorn. But there are divergences of detail which deserve

* See his letter, *Athenæum*, February 7, 1891.

careful investigation, towards which the accompanying table will prove of service.

The first thing to observe is that the Arabic form clearly constitutes the bridge between the Occident and Orient on this occasion. Alone of the Western versions it preserves "The Bees,"* which exist in the two Indian forms, while already it shows the Western change of the Indian elephant into the nondescript dragon. We may conclude from this that the Arabic does not derive from the Greek, and is closer to the Indian original than it.

A still more remarkable parallel exists to this parable in the far-famed Norse Legend of the *Yggdrasil*.† This is a giant ash, whose branches spread round the world. Its three roots are connected with Heaven, Earth, and Hell: under each root gushes a well-spring; from the tree trickles a fall of honey. On its

---

* They occur, however, without allegorical significance, in the Hebrew form of the *Bidpai*. Cf. Steinschneider, *Übersetzungen*, p. 880, who has a mass of information on this parable.

† I give this description from Grimm, *Teutonic Mythology*, 796. Unfortunately he does not give any references, and some of the details are missing from the account given in the *Grimmis-Mal* in Vigfusson and York-Powell, *Corp. Poet. Bor.*, i. 73.

TABLE.

Objects.	Mahab.	Jaina.	Avadanas.	Bidpai.	Bilauhar.	Barlaam.
Well	Body	Human Life	{ Human Dwelling	World	World	World.
Tree	{ Hope of Life	Life	Root of Life	—	Life	—
Serpent	Time	Under-World	Hell	—	—	—
Four Heads	—	Passions	Elements	Humours	Humours	Elements.
Mice	{ Day and Night	Full and New Moon	Sun and Moon	{ Day and Night	Day and Night	Day and Night.
Elephant	Year	Death	Death	Death	Death	Hell
Honey	{ Pleasure of Senses	Pleasure of Senses	Pleasure	Pleasure	Pleasure	Pleasure.
Bees	Desires	Illnesses	—	—	Troubles	—

topmost bough sits an eagle, while a snake is gnawing at its roots. A squirrel runs up and down, trying to create enmity between the snake and the eagle, and round the tree are four stags. Most of these animals have names given them which are clearly of allegorical or mythological significance. At first sight there is remarkable similarity, at least in the accessories of the two conceptions—the tree itself, the trickling honey, the gnawed root, and the four stags.

Much resemblance, however, disappears on closer examination. The central ideas of the two legends are entirely diverse. One is cosmological, the other eschatological.* As Grimm observes, "the only startling thing is the agreement in certain accessories" (*Teut. Myth.*, 799). Yet this resemblance in accessories is the more striking on that account. M. Bédier has recently suggested a formula for testing the derivation of folktales and legends from one another. He separates the central idea of a story from the accidental accessories. He expresses the former by ω, and the details by a, b, c, d, &c. His contention is, that mere

---

* There is, however, reference to Hell, at least in the serpent and the gnawed root of the Norse version.

resemblance in the central idea (ω) does not prove derivation, but that resemblance in the details (a, b, c, d, &c.) does do so. Thus, if two stories be represented by the formulæ ω + a + b + c + d and ω + e + f + g + h, we cannot conclude that the latter is derived from the former. The method is not so rigid or so objective as M. Bédier imagines. There is a good deal of elasticity and possibility of subjective preference in his ω. But be that as it may, on the present occasion we have a state of affairs which has not been contemplated in M. Bédier's scheme. The ω is different, while some of the details are the same. We get the formulæ—

Yggdrasil   = ω + a + b + c + d + e + f
Man in Well = ξ + a + b + c + d + g + h

If the central idea had been in both cases the same there could be no doubt as to the derivative character of the myth of Yggdrasil, according to M. Bédier's method and formula. As it is, we are met by a state of affairs which, so far as I can observe, has not been contemplated by M. Bédier, and various interpretations will be given to the resemblance of details by various people. For myself, I am inclined to think that the Yggdrasil Myth has been "contaminated" by the other mediæval allegory of the "Man in the Well." In the first place, the accessories common to the two are, in large measure, meaningless in the Yggdrasil Myth, especially "The Four Stags"; in the second place, the Norse Myth, so far from being primitive, as Grimm regards it, is probably late and artificial. Messrs. Vigfusson and York-Powell, indeed, go so far as to suggest that the Myth never "travelled beyond the single poem in which it was wrought out by a Master-Mind" (*Corp. Poet. Bor.*, ii. 459). As for the possibility of the Barlaam Legend reaching Iceland, one may remember the close connection between Norway and Constantinople through the Varangars, the Norse bodyguard of the Eastern Emperors. Altogether, therefore, I think it possible, and even likely, that the Yggdrasil Myth, in the form in which we have it now, has been influenced in some of its details by the parable of the "Man in the Well." *

Before leaving this interesting parable some-

---

* It is fair to add that Professor Bugge, who is generally most ready to account for such similarities by transmission, does not see how to do so in the present instance. See his *Studien*.

thing should be said as to its pictorial representations. In most of the illustrated editions of the *Bidpai* the illustration of this parable is given; one will be found, *e.g.*, in my edition of the first English version of the *Bidpai* in this series, p. 61. Quite at the other end of the world the "Man in the Well" can be found illustrated in a Chinese chap-book dealing with the story, which is described and figured in the *Royal Asiatic Society Journal*, China Branch, XIX. i. 94. The parable also formed the subject for church decoration, and it is still to be found on the walls of several Italian churches. We have here a further example of that migration of illustrations to which I referred in a former volume of this series (*Bidpai*, pp. xix.-xxiv.).

4. *The Three Friends.*—This parable is remarkable for the number of dramatic versions to which it has given rise. But before discussing these it is worth while referring to the possibility that this parable reached the West from the East before the *Barlaam* was composed. There is, indeed, a somewhat similar parable, given by Petrus Alfonsi, a Spanish Jewish convert of the early twelfth century, in

which a man tests the fidelity of his friend by pretending to be a murderer. The sources of Alfonsi are, in every case, Oriental, yet the same anecdote is told by Polyænus, a writer of the second century, as occurring to Alcibiades. While, however, the central idea of this story is the same as that of the *Barlaam*, its details are different, and so, according to M. Bédier's principle, we cannot count them as connected by transmission. But in a Jewish work, *Pirke R. Eleazar*, c. xliii., the parable occurs in nearly the same form as the *Barlaam*.* The opening words of the story are sufficient to indicate this: "Man has, during life, three friends. These are—his children, his money, and his good works." It is generally thought that this work was composed in the sixth century A.D., just before the *Barlaam* commenced its long travels from Persia. And if so, it might be thought possible that the Jewish form of the Legend was the original one, especially as its moral is pointed by appropriate Biblical verses. Yet in the *Barlaam* it occurs in the Arabic,

* There seem to be a reference to this in the sixth or supplementary chapter of the *Pirke Aboth*. But this chapter is, according to Dr. Taylor, its latest and best editor, quite a recent addendum.

Georgian, and Greek versions, so that it was almost certainly in the Indian original. Either, therefore, that original got to the West, or at least to Syria or Babylon, independently, or the form of the story in the *Pirke Eleazar* was derived from the *Barlaam*, and its composition must therefore be later than the seventh century. Of its wide spread through the *Barlaam* there is no doubt. It found a place in all the great mediæval collections, like the *Gesta Romanorum*, and even in Stainhöwel's Äsop (*cf.* my edition of Caxton, ii. p. 206).

Of its popularity in England an interesting proof was afforded by a Morality founded upon the parable, written in the fifteenth and printed in the early sixteenth century by John Scott, a pupil of Pynson's (*circa* 1592). This Morality, entitled *Every Man*, was translated into Latin by Christian Sterk, and printed in 1548 under the title *Homulus*; while a Dutch poet, Peter van Diest, obtained a prize for a Dutch version of the same title, which was printed at Cologne in 1536. Dr. Goedeke, from whose monograph[*] I take the above items, is of opinion that the English version was the source of the Conti-

[*] *Every Man; Homulus und Hekastus.* Hanover, 1865.

nental ones. Dr. Logeman, on the contrary, considers the Dutch version the source of the subsequent ones. I will not attempt to decide when such doctors disagree, but will merely remark that Academic dramas on the same theme continued to be composed by Continental scholars throughout the seventeenth century. These plays, whose titles are given by Dr. Goedeke, form, perhaps, the most striking proof of the popularity of the parable of *Barlaam*.

5. *Man and Bird.*—The story of the man who caught a nightingale and let it go on promise of receiving three pieces of advice is well known in English Literature as having formed the subject of one of Lydgate's pieces, and is equally well known in Germany, being the subject of a version by Wieland. Its earliest appearance is in the Barlaam Literature, but it also occurs in the very early *Disciplina Clericalis* of Petrus Alfonsi. It is, of course, possible that the Spanish convert got the allegory from *Barlaam*, but we know that several other of his allegories were derived from Eastern oral sources. It is, therefore, possible that he obtained the Legend of the "Man and Bird" from some other derivative of the Indian original. That it had an Indian

original would almost be proven by the fact that it occurs in all the four earliest versions, Arabic, Georgian, Hebrew, and Greek. Benfey (in his *Einleitung*, p. 380) compares the Indian story of the bird who promises a hunter some treasure if he will release him, and goes on to point out that in some Indian stories a piece of advice is often regarded as equal to treasure-trove. These indications serve only to show that the story is not inconsistent with Indian ideas. But, on the other hand, there is nothing specifically Indian in those ideas. But for the fact that the story occurs for the first time in the *Barlaam* we could not be certain of its Indian origin. But it must be remembered that when we prove the Indian *provenance* of some of the tales in the book, this adds considerably to the weight of probability of the same origin in cases where we can only indicate probability. As I have elsewhere remarked, the strength of the chain of tradition depends on that of its strongest link, though this be against the catenary laws of physicists.

6. *Language of Animals.*—This story only occurs in one of the early versions of *Barlaam*, the Hebrew *Prince and Dervish*. But the

f

story is remarkable as occurring as a widespread folktale. Mr. Fraser, who discusses it in connection with a general inquiry into the folk-belief in the "Language of Animals" (*Arch. Rev.*, i. 168-72), quotes Servian, Indian, Arabic, Italian, Annamite, Tartar, and Finnish versions. He does not, however, refer to the Hebrew one, though this is, undoubtedly, the earliest extant. Yet it is impossible to consider the Hebrew the source of the folktales, and it can, therefore, only be regarded as one of the somewhat rare cases in which folktales have been taken up into Literature. It may be worth while to devote some consideration to this folktale, as an instance of the problem of diffusion.

Nobody, not even M. Bédier, would assert that such a complex and artificial story as this could have been invented casually and independently on two different occasions. A man learns the language of animals on condition he does not betray his knowledge. On one occasion he bursts into laughter on hearing some animal speak, and is pestered by his wife to tell her why he laughed. He answers that he must die if he tells her. But this, naturally, only increases her curiosity and persistence.

He is about to give way, when he hears other animals rebuking him for his weakness. *They know how to rule their wives; why should not he?* A judicious application of the stick cures the wife of her curiosity.

Such are the main outlines of the story, and one may be pretty confident that it was only invented once. The chief variation occurs with regard to the species of animal that gives the advice by which the man extricates himself from his difficulties. In the Hebrew and in the *Arabian Nights*, as well as in all the European versions, the Counsellor is a Cock, who points out that, if he can rule a hundred hens, he does not see why the man cannot overcome a single wife. In two of the Indian versions, and in the Annamite Story, it is an Ant who gives the advice. It is probable that Mohammed knew this version, and refers to it in the Koran in the Sura entitled *Ant*. (Vulgate 27, Nöldeke-Rodwell, 68). Finally, the Tamul, Jaina, and Turkish versions, given by Benfey, and a further Indian version, which Mr. Fraser quotes from Bastian, make the Counsellor a He-goat. This criterion would give us three lines of derivation from the original. Considering the popularity of the *Arabian Nights*, it might, naturally, be supposed that the European versions, in which we are mostly interested, came from that source. But the two Italian versions of Morlini and Straparola were printed in the sixteenth century, long before Galland had made the *Arabian Nights* popular. So that it is impossible to regard the latter as the source of the European versions. These must have spread from the East by the folk and through the folk. But that they did spread thence there can be but little doubt in the mind of any one who compares the evidence.

7. *The Robbers' Nemesis.*—Here again we have a tale only occurring in the Hebrew *Barlaam*, and yet certainly derived from India. That it is the source of Chaucer's *Pardonere's Tale* makes it of exceptional interest. It is, also, curious to find that the story, which, in its original form, is told of the Buddha, was, later on, told about Jesus. The original was discovered by Dr. Morris in the *Vedabha Jataka*, the forty-eighth Birth-Story of Buddha (*The Jataka*, tr. Chalmers, vol. i. pp. 121-4). Here Buddha foresees the Nemesis

which will befall the robbers. In a poetical Persian version, and in two Arabic versions, given by Mr. Clouston in the Chaucer Society's *Originals*, pp. 423-9, it is Jesus, Son of Mary, who has the prophetic insight of the Nemesis.

This story is only found among the folk in Germany, where it was, possibly, made popular by Hans Sachs. In Italy it formed the subject of a Miracle Play, but, so far as I know, it does not occur among the Italian folktales; while the Portuguese version, given by Braga, is not a true folktale, but is reproduced from a Portuguese writer of the fourteenth century. Thus the story is not a true folktale, and its diffusion has been entirely literary.

8. *King, Man, and Skull.*—In the Bombay, Arabic, and in one of the Persion versions occurs the well-known story of *Alexander and the Skull*, though the great Conqueror's name is not mentioned. "A little dust will cover the eye that took in the whole world in its glance." This *memento mori* is mentioned in the Talmud about Alexander, and recalls other anecdotes given in Plutarch's Life. It may, therefore, be a Greek tradition about the great Conqueror, and is, clearly enough, an inter-

polation in the Barlaam Literature. But its existence in one form of it is a proof that interpolations of parables were possible, and should make us careful before assuming that any one parable was in the Indian original unless literary criticism can establish its *provenance*.

9. *Man among Ghouls.* — In the Bombay Arabic there occurs an interpolated story of a vessel that was cast ashore on an island inhabited by ghouls, who disguise themselves as beautiful maidens. This has a certain amount of similarity with the *Myth of the Sirens*, while it has several Indian and Buddhistic variants (for which see Appendix. II.), which prove that it was a favourite conception of the Buddhists. Indeed, the ghoul who disguises herself as a beautiful maiden is quite a frequent *motif* in Indian folktales. The chief interest of the story is, however, its relation to the incident in the Odyssey. It has to be remembered that the Bishop of Colombo is inclined to think that certain portions of the *Jatakas* have been influenced by the general scheme of the Odyssey.*
It, therefore, becomes possible that, instead of the Sirens being derived from the Ghouls in

* *Journ. R. A. S.*, Ceylon branch.

this instance, the relationship may be of an inverse kind. The early date of the Odyssey makes it practically impossible that Homer could have been influenced by any transmission from India. On the other hand, resemblance of the two legends is not so close as to force us to assume derivation on either side.

10. *Women as Demons.*—The lad who had never seen a woman, and was told the first one he saw was a demon, yet prefers the demon to anything else he had seen, is almost the only parable of *Barlaam* which has any humour in it. It is a distinctly Indian conception, though it chimed in sufficiently with the Christian view of the wickedness of woman to be very popular among the mediæval preachers. It occurs in both of the great Indian books, the *Mahabharata* and the *Ramayana*, so that its Indian origin is undoubted. Indeed, it is one of the points requiring further investigation whether the conception of the innate wickedness of woman, which forms a stock subject of Christian homiletics, was not derived from the similar Buddhistic conception. Some time ago Dr. Donaldson showed, in the *Contemporary Review* (September 1889), that the de-

graded conception of the nature of woman current in early Christianity could not be traced to either Jewish or classical influence. It is one of the many instances in which the legend and doctrines of Christianity and Buddhism show such a remarkable resemblance that we are tempted, on folklore principles, to assume some Indian influence.

These are all the Parables of Barlaam which seem to me to require special comment, beyond the information given in the notes to Appendix II. The resemblance of one of the remaining parables to the *Ballad of King Cophetua*, and of another to Dryden's *Cimon and Iphigenia*, are merely casual, and are of only secondary interest from the folklore standpoint. But these, and others given in Appendix II., will not be found uninteresting by readers who care for good stories. I cannot flatter myself that anything I can say will be as interesting to the reader as the text of the parables given in Appendix II. After reading them the reader will be able more fully to understand their widespread popularity throughout mediæval Europe, to which we now turn.

V

Barlaam in Europe

Of the wide extent to which the *Barlaam* was translated in the European languages no better evidence could be afforded than the pedigree in which I have attempted to sum up Dr. Kuhn's elaborate bibliographical lists of translations and versions. These number no less than sixty separate translations, many of which have gone through very many editions. From Italy to Iceland, from Spain to Russia, there is scarcely a land or a language into which *Barlaam* has not penetrated. Even in the distant Philippines, it will be seen from the pedigree, a Tagol version was made from the Spanish and printed at Manilla in 1712. Even the Fables of Bidpai have scarcely attained to such œcumenical diffusion.

Restricting ourselves to Europe, we find that it is chiefly the patronage of the Church that has given rise to so extensive a literature. It was because they were thought to be saintly exemplars that the lives of Barlaam and Josaphat became such an object of interest to all good Catholics. It is, accordingly, the versions in the sacred language of the Church which have, as a rule, the largest number of derivates. Europe read the Parables of Barlaam, for the most part, in Latin.

There are two Latin versions which have been the main source of the European adaptations of the Legend. The earlier one, attributed to one Anatasius Bibliothecarius, went into French, German, English, Spanish, Icelandic, Irish, and Czech, through the medium of the *Vitæ Sanctorum*, into which it had been received.* Some of these adaptations of the First Latin had themselves vigorous offshoots. Thus, the Icelandic gave birth to Danish and Swedish *Barlaams*. Solorzano's Spanish version was done into Portuguese, and had the still greater honour of being made the foundation of a drama by Lope de Vega. This drama, in its turn, was one of the sources

---

* For details, see pedigree, which summarises Dr. Kuhn's bibliographical lists.

of Calderon's most famous play *La Vida es Sueño.**

One of the French versions was even more prolific. Executed in prose in the thirteenth century, it got into Provençal and became the father of the numerous Italian offshoots which include a mediæval sacred drama, and another drama, not perhaps so sacred, by Pulci.

This First Latin version, as received into the *Vitæ Sanctorum*, was also taken up into two great mediæval collections which thus helped to spread the Barlaam Legend and Parables. St. Vincent of Beauvais placed an abstract of it in his huge Encyclopædia in the historical section (*Speculum Historialæ*, xv.). Another abstract was included by Jacobus de Voragine in his *Golden Legend*, whence it was utilised to form the subject of two French Miracle Plays, while the book itself got into English in Caxton's version, which we have repeated in this volume.

Besides the Caxton, there are no less than four mediæval English versions, which have

* See Mr. Maccoll's *Select Plays of Calderon*, pp. 121-23.

recently been printed under the editorial care of Dr. Horstmann. Three in verse were included by him in his *Altenglische Legenden* (Paderborn, 1875), and one in prose printed by him in a programme in 1877.* None of these English versions give either the Legend or the Parables in a particularly attractive form, and, for the most part, when we can trace any influence of the Barlaam Literature in England it is, probably, directly due to one of the Latin versions of the Legend, or to the adaptations of the Parables used as *Exempla* by English monks, like Nicholas Bozon.† When one refers to the chapbook versions, one of which is reprinted in this volume, the short and simple annals of the English *Barlaam* are concluded.

There yet remains another Latin version

---

* I am indebted to Dr. Kölbing for an opportunity of seeing this latter, which is rather rare. It has accordingly been omitted by the Rev. J. Morrison, who has reprinted the three metrical versions as an Appendix to Dr. Macdonald's *Story of Barlaam and Josaphat* (Calcutta, 1895, Thacker). The volume also contains *The History of the Five Wise Philosophers*.

† See *Contes moralisés* de Nicole Bozon: edit. Toulmin Smith and Meyer, pp. 46, 59, 106, and corresponding Notes. *Cf.* Jacques de Vitry, *Exempla:* edit. Crane, Nos. ix., xxxviii., xlii., xlvii., lxxviii., lxxxii., cx., cxxxiv.

which had considerable influence upon the spread of the *Barlaam*. When Abbot Billius of S. Michel in Britanny produced a Latin edition of the works of John of Damascus, he became dissatisfied with the early Latin version and executed one of his own, which appeared in the Saint's *Opera*, Paris, 1577, and separately, sixteen years afterwards. This gave rise to further French translations, and to Dutch, Polish, and Spanish adaptations. This last had the distinction of being adopted into the Tagol dialect of Manilla, and was received into a Spanish "Golden Legend" known as the *Flos Sanctorum*, which was translated back into Latin, as well as into French, Italian, German, Dutch, and English.

There remain only to be considered the Slavonic versions which spread through East Europe. These all derive from the Old Slavonic, which forms the basis of the modern Russian, and of various Roumanian versions. The Legend has taken firm root in Slavonic soil, and has given rise, both in Russia and Roumania, to a most pathetic folksong in which Josaphat is represented addressing the wilderness in which he is to pass his ascetic life.* It is, doubtless, from one of the popular Russian versions that Count Tolstoi has obtained his knowledge of the *Barlaam*, of which he gives evidence in his *Confessions*.

The œcumenical spread of the Barlaam Literature, which I have now sufficiently indicated by this summary of the bibliography of the book—though this has, of course, to be supplemented by the evidence of the separate spread of the Parables—is sufficient proof of the attractiveness both of Legend and Parables to the mediæval mind of Europe. When we ask what is the charm which attracted mediæval Christendom to what is, after all, only a version of the life and parables of Buddha, the answer is not far to seek. The world has known, up till now, four great systems of Religion: Paganism, Buddhism, Christianity, and Culture, of which last Goethe may be described as the High Priest. Paganism in its various forms may be most simply described as the Worship of the Social Bond. All the other three religions have for their main object the salvation of the individual. And all three are at one as

---

* *Cf.* Castor, *Lit. Pop. Rom.*, pp. 46-53; and Kuhn's References, p. 53.

to the means of salvation. "*Entbehren, entbehren sollst du*," cried Goethe, and in his own way was only repeating what Buddha and Christ had said before him. Renunciation as the key of salvation is thus the teaching of all modern religions. It is because the Barlaam Legend, and many of its Parables, have presented renunciation as the ideal of man's striving, that it came home in the Middle Ages so persistently to the folk with whom renunciation is a necessity of existence. The truth embodied in this tale has indeed come home to lowly minds.

APPENDIX I.

ABSTRACT OF LEGEND

[The following abstract gives the main results of the restoration of the original legend made from the various early versions, not derived from the Greek, by Kuhn, pp. 15-33. I have run his §§ 3 and 4 into one, so that after 3, his sections are numbered one higher than mine. In the annotations, Arab. references to the pages of the Bombay *Kitâb.*, Gr. to the pages of Boissonade's Greek text, Heb. references to the chapters ("Gates") of Ibn Chisdai. For parables, see Appendix II.]

I.—BARLAAM.

There lived once a king in India mighty and powerful, who knew not the true faith, and persecuted grievously its adherents. Now he had no son to follow him, and this grieved him sorely. One night his chief wife dreamed that a huge white elephant came down to her from the air, but injured her not. The astrologers declared to the king that he would have a son.

[Arab. 3-5. Gr. 1-8. Heb. Int. The name of the king is in Arab. *Janaisar*, in Georg. *Iabenes*, in Gr. *Abenner*. (Cf. 2 Sam. iii. 6.) The name of the country in Arab. is Shawilabatt, a reminiscence of Kapilavastu. The dream only in Arabic, but certainly in original, owing to Buddhistic parallels. (Cf. Beal, *Rom. Leg.* 37.)]

II.

The King learnt that one of his chief men had been converted to the true faith, and summoned him to him. The Sage told him of the vanity of the world, and besought him to humble his pride: but the King was incensed, and drove the Sage from his kingdom.

[Arab. 5-17. Gr. 8-18. Heb. i.-iii. The sermon on the vanity of the world much contracted in Gr. Part of it is found later, Gr. 109-11.]

III.

A son is born to the King, who is named Yudâsaf, and when his horoscope is cast the astrologers declare, that while he would surpass all his forebears in majesty, he would turn to the true faith. So the King built for him a beautiful palace far away from the haunts of men, so that he could never know the common lot of men or learn the nature of death.

Meanwhile he continued the strictest persecution of the followers of the faith.

> [Arab. 17-27. Gr. 18-28. Heb. iv. v. Name of Prince in Georg. *Iodasap*, in Arab. *Búdásaf*. K. considers latter only accidentally identical with Arabic title of Buddha.]

IV.

Meanwhile the Prince grows up and begins to feel the loneliness of his position. He asks his teachers, and learns the secret of his imprisonment. Thereupon he begs his father to grant him greater freedom: but when he goes out he meets a blind man, and a leper, and an old man, and a corpse, and learns from these the common fate of man. Who shall give him consolation for the fate that awaits him? he asks, and is told that only the hermits of the true faith can allay the fear of death. These have been driven from the country.

> [Arab. 27-34. Gr. 28-35. Heb. vi. Name of the Teacher not given in Gr. or Arab., but *Zandani* in Georg. (Cf. Chandaka, Buddha's Charioteer.) Arab. alone adds a Buddhistic trait, as follows: "An astrologer declares that the boy will forsake the world, unless he is made to shed blood. The lad is put to sacrifice a sheep, but instead, wounds himself in his left hand, and faints." (Cf. the Buddhistic Ahinsa.) For the meetings, cf. Carus, *Gospel of Buddha*, § vi., and *supra*, pp. xliv.-v.]

V.

Now the holy hermit Barlaam came at this time to the court of the Prince in the garb of a merchant, and came into his presence under the pretext that he had precious stones to show him. When asked what it is, he tells the tale of:—

V.a. *The Holy King and the Hermit,*

which includes also the parables—

    V.a. i. *The Trumpet of Death.*
    V.a. ii. *The Four Caskets.*
    V.a. iii. *The Sower.*

[Arab. 37-46. Gr. 36-44. Heb. vii,-viii. Gr. puts *Parable of Sower* first. For parables, see *infra*. Heb. adds in c. ix. that of V.b., *Bird and Fisherman*.]

VI.

Barlaam teaches the vanity of this world by means of the three parables—

    VI.a. *The Man in the Well.*
    VI.b. *The Three Friends.*
    VI.c. *The King of the Year.*

[Arab. 47-69. Gr. 44-120, but with much Christian interpolations (Biblical History, 44-56; the Sacrament of Baptism, 58-9, 88-9, Old and New Testament, 90-2, Repentance, 90-4, Martyrs and Monks, 100-8). None of these in Georg., which, however, contains the Christian Confession of Faith, Gr. 83-4. Other Christian interpolations in Gr. 126-134. Heb. x.-xiv., adding the *Parable of the Cannibal King*, also found in Arab., which has besides the Apologues, *Dogs and Carrion. Bird and Prophet, Sun of Wisdom, King and Shepherd,*

VII.

The Prince then inquires why his father should have persecuted the followers of the true faith if their doctrines were so sound. Barlaam tells the parables—

VII.a. *The Heathen King and the Believing Vizier.*
(VII.a. i. *The Swimmer and his Comrades.*)
VII.b. *The Rich Young Man and the Beggar's Daughter.*
(VII.b. ii. *Education by Love*).
VII.c. *The Man and the Bird.*

The Prince asks Barlaam how old he is, and is told "twelve years old," for only during the time of hermithood had he truly lived.

> [Arab. 39-117. Gr. 134-143. But *Man and Bird* in § vi. In Gr. Barlaam has lived 45 out of 70 years: in Georg. 18 out of 60. Heb. xvi.-xxii., adding in xxi. *The Prophet and the Bird, The Language of Animals,* and *The Robbers' Nemesis.*]

VIII.

The Prince's guardian, Zardan, overhears the conversation of Barlaam and Yudâsaf, and threatens to tell the King, but is induced not to do so by the Prince.

> [Arab. 117-23, Gr. 179-83 (before end of § ix.), Heb. xxiv. and portions of xxv., xxvi., but from henceforth pursues an original course till end of xxxv. (= § ix.). Georg. omits Christian dogmatics of Gr. 180-1.]

IX.

Barlaam tells the Prince that he must leave him, whereupon the Prince expresses his willingness to go with him. Then Barlaam tells the parable—

IX.a. *The Tame Gazelle.*

The Prince inquires after the mode of life and dress of the followers of the true faith, which Barlaam shows to him. Thereupon the Prince exchanges clothes with Barlaam, who goes his way.

> [Arab. 123-35. Gr. 154-160, but with transposition of incidents. Then 161-178, Joasaph's Baptism and First Communion. Georg. omits 161-3 (Confession of Faith), 165-6 (Mass), 166-7 (Images and Cross), 167 (Heretics), 167-8 (Baptism and Communion). Then follows in Gr. 179-83 (§ viii.). Then 183-9 (Exchange of Clothes and Parting). There is a Buddhistic analogy for the exchange of clothes in that of Buddha and Mahakasyapa. (Cf. Beal, *Rom. Leg.* 145-318.)]

X.

The King learns through Zardan the conversion of his son, and consults with his astrologer, Araches. He recommends, either to seize Barlaam and put him to death, or if he cannot be found, to get a stranger, named Nachor, to personate him and be overcome in a public disputation upon the faith.

> [Arab. 135-48. Gr. 190-205. Arab. has only one *Rakis*, who is sliced by Gr. and Georg. into two, Araches and Nachor. Kuhn sees in Rakis some reminiscence of the Buddhistic Devadatta.]

XI.

Before the disputation the King tries twice to turn his son from the New Way. At first with menaces, and then with persuasive mildness.

> [Arab. 148-236. Gr. 206-32. Arab. has two discussions: in course of second, the Prince enumerates his ancestors and declares they were all followers of al-Budd. Both King and son agree as to the beauty of al-Budd's doctrines. Hence Kuhn sees an interpolation from the *Kitâb al-Budd.*]

XII.

The disputation is held, but beforehand the Prince threatens Nachor to tear him asunder if he does not conquer for the right faith. Nachor triumphs and flees into the wilderness.

> [Arab. 236-48. Gr. 232-62, but with the insertion of *The Apology of Aristides.*]

XIII.

The magician, Theudas, recommends the King to lead the Prince away by the wiles of woman, and narrates the parable—

XIII.a. *The Youth who had never seen a Woman.*

The Prince resists temptation and sees in a dream the fate of the saints and the damned. He reproaches the King, and remains firm to the true faith. He also interviews Theudas, and tells him the parable—

XIII.b. *The Peacock and the Raven.*

Theudas is converted to the true faith, and the Prince goes forth into the wilderness to live a hermit's life with Barlaam.

[Arab. 249–70. Gr. 263–302. Heb. xxxv. Georg. adds parable, *Man and Amorous Wife*, and omits Christian interpolations of Gr. 286–9 (Against Idolatry), 290–2 (Incarnation), 293–6 (Spread of Christianity), 297–9 (Controversy of Heathen Philosophers and Poets).

The magician is called *T'edam* in Georg., *Tahdam* in Arab., but *Theudas* in Gr. (Cf. Acts v. 37.) In Arab. the Prince is saved from temptation by a dream, and converts Tahdam by the parable of *Peacock and Raven* to the faith of al-Budd, and tells the Prince that forty years before he had met a wise Indian who had told him that al-Budd had told that parable 300 years before, and prophesied that the true Peacock would come after 300 years.

The temptation is Buddhistic. (Cf. Rhys Davids, *Birth Stories*, i. 81, and Carus, *Gospel of Buddha*, § xi.) Theudas represents Buddha's schoolfellow, Udayin. (Beal, p. 349.) The parable is the *Baveru Jataka*. In Gr. and Georg. the King becomes converted, and after his death Joasaph puts another on the throne, and joins Barlaam in the wilderness. Both saints die, and their relics are collected. In Arab. II. the Prince flees by night from his palace together with his vizier. He is stopped by a beautiful boy, who tries to induce him to remain. But he continues his flight on horseback, and when he arrives at the edge of the wilderness sends the vizier back with his horse and valuables. He then sees a great tree by a brook. On the tree grow fruit that thanked him as he plucked them. Four angels take him up to heaven, where he is taught of wisdom, and then returns to earth, and converts all he meets. He visits his native town and his father, and at last reaches Kashmir, where he puts his head to the west, and his feet to the east, and dies after giving his blessing to his favourite pupil *Anand*. Here we have clearly the Great Renunciation, and the enlightenment under the Bo-Tree. The vizier is *Chandaka*, the boy, *Rahula*. Kashmir is a misreading for *Kusinara*, and Anand, of *Ananda*. (Cf. Carus, §§ vii., xi., xcvi., xcvii.)]

APPENDIX II.

[The following series of abstracts give the parables contained in the early versions of the Barlaam, with bibliographical index of their occurrences elsewhere, as well as references with previous critical treatment of the separate parables. For the Greek I have referred to Zotenberg's edition of the parable at the end of the *Notice* (Z). For the Halle Arabic I have referred to the translation by Mr. Rehatsek in the *Journ. Roy. Asiat. Soc.*, N.S., xxii. 119–55 (Reh.), for a translation of the Greek to Mr. R. Chambers' English version, *ibid.* xxiii. (C.), and Lubrecht's German (L.). For the Hebrew I give the "gate" or chapter, while for the Georgian and the other Arabic versions Kuhn and Hommel are my authorities. To each parable I have added a Roman numeral indicating the section of the original in which it is inserted. (See App. I.) Under the heading "Literature" I have mainly confined myself to the more recent monographs, which themselves contain references to earlier treatments.]

II.a. *Anger and Passion.*

To embrace the true faith it is necessary to send away its enemies. And what are they? Anger and Desire. These may support the truly human being who directs his life according to the Spirit, but for carnal beings they are deadly enemies.

[Z. i., L. p. 8, C. 425.]

V.a. *The Trumpet of Death and the Four Caskets.*

Z. v., vi., L. p. 35, C. 433.

A king once saw two hermits clad in scanty clothing passing by his state carriage. He leapt out, and bowed down before them and saluted them with every mark of respect and honour. His courtiers could not make anything of this, and asked the King's younger brother to remonstrate with him at his behaviour. This he did: but next day the King sent to him a herald with the Trumpet of Death, with which it was customary in that country to announce to high-born criminals that they were condemned to death. The Prince in great dismay went weeping to the King, and begged to know in what he had offended. The King replied, "In naught, my brother, but I will teach thee why I greeted the hermits so respectfully. If thou art so moved at seeing the herald of thy own brother, should I not be even more impressed at seeing the herald of my God?" And so saying he dismissed his brother. But he caused four caskets to be made: two covered with gold and precious stones, but containing naught but dry bones. The other two, however, he covered only with clay, but filled them with jewels and costly pearls. He then summoned the courtiers to him and asked them to give judgment as to the value of the caskets. They replied that those covered with gold must contain the royal jewels, while the clay could be of no particular value. Thereupon the King ordered the caskets to be opened, and pointing to the golden ones he said, "These represent the men who go about clothed in fine raiment but within are full of evil deeds. But these," he added, turning to the caskets of clay, "represent those holy men who, though ill clad, are full of jewels of the faith."

[DEATH TRUMPET.—*Occurrence in Barlaam Literature.*—See App. I., v. Occurring in Arab., Georg., and Gr., it must have been in Indian original, and was probably there also connected with "The Four Caskets." Nearly all the derivates of the Greek contain it.

Indian Original.—Legend of Asoka's brother, Vitasoka (Burnouf, *Introd.*). (Cf. *Katha-sarit-sagara*, VI. xvii., tr. Tawney, i. 237.)

Parallels.—The Sword of Damocles (Cicero, *Tusc. Disp.*, v. 21; Oesterley on *Gesta*, 143; *Wendenmuth*, ii. 21; Crane on *Exempla*, xlii.b).

Derivates.—Jacques de Vitry, *Exempla*, ed. Crane, xlii.; Paratus, *Sermones*, 145; Wright, *Latin Stories*, 103; John of Bromyard, s.v. "Homo"; *Gesta Romanorum*, ed. Oesterley, 143; *Abundancia exemp.*, f. 30.b; Gower, *Conf. Amant.* (Cf. Swan, *Gesta*, 401); *Mag. speculum exemp.*, ed. 1610, s.v. Judicium; *Libro de enxemplos*, 121, 223; Brit. Mus. MS., add. 11,284, ff. 27b, 40b (Crane).

Literature.—E. Braunholtz. *Die Erste Nichtchristliche, Parabel des Barlaam und Josaphat, ihre Herkunft und Verbreitung*, Halle, 1884, but mainly concerned with *Four Caskets*. For reviews, &c., see that parable s.v. *Literature*; Oesterley on *Gesta*, 143; *Wendenmuth.*, ii. 21. (But confusing with Damocles) Crane, *ut supra*; Cassell, *Aus Literatur und Symbolik*, 166-8; Kuhn, 74-5.

THE FOUR CASKETS.—*Occurrences in Barlaam.*—In Arab., Georg., and Gr., therefore in original. In all derivates of Gr.

Indian Original.—Tale of Asoka's Minister Yasas. (Burnouf, *Introd.*, 333; St. Hilaire, *Bouddha*, 105.) With the addition of "The Caskets," from Buddhistic "Folk-Tales," on which Benfey, *Pants*, i. 407 seq.

Parallels.—Buddhistic comparison of man's body to a casket (*Lalita Vistara*, tr. Foucaux, p. 358). Cf. Gospel parallel of Whited Sepulchres and Talmudic Legends, *Baba Bathra*, 58a; *Synhedrin*, 108b. (Cf. Gaster, *Beiträge*, pp. 6-10.) For Folk-Tales containing choice of Caskets, see Cosquin, *l.c.*

Derivates.—Vincentius Bellovacensis, *Spec. hist.*, xv. 10; *Gerard de Roussillon*, ed. Michel; *Legenda aurea*, f. 138b, and offshoots; Guy de Cambrai, *Barlaam*, ed. Zotenberg and Meyer, p. 37; Jehan de Condé, "Dou roi et des hiermittes" in *Dits et Contes*, ed. Scheler., II. i. 63; Bartsch, *Provenz. Lesebuch*, 166-74; Storia de' SS. *Barlaam e Giosafatte*, ed. Bottari, Rome, 1734, p. 20; *Vita di Giosafatte* in Bini, *Rime e prosa*, Lucca, 1852, p. 124; Boccaccio, *Decamerone*, x. 1; Gower, *Confessio Amantis*, ed. Pauli, ii. 203; Morlini, nov. v.; Straparola, *Notti*, fav. v.; Carion, *Chronica*, 1533, f. 2013b (Kaiser Sigmund, see Genealogy for offshoots); Bromyard, *Summa Prædicantium*, s.v. "Honor"; *Gesta Romanorum*, ed. Oesterley, 251, ed. Herrtage, p. 294; Shakespeare, *Merchant of Venice*, ii. 1, 7, 9; iii. 2; Jacques de Vitry, *Exempla*, ed. Crane, xlvii.; Bozon, *Contes moralisés*, ed. Toulmin Smith and Meyer, lxxxiv.

Literature.—Braunholtz, *ut supra*. (Cf. Reviews by Zingarelli, *Arch. Tradiz. Popol*, iii. 143-6; Brandes, *Anglia*, viii. 24-6; Varnhagen, *Deuts. Lit. Zeit.* 1885,

p. 17; *Giorn. Lett. Ital.*, iii. 142; Bolte, *Jahresber. German. Philol.*, vi. 116); Simrock, *Quellen*, iii. 201; Landau, *Quellen;* Benfey, *Pants*, i. 407; Oesterley, Herrtage, Crane, 11, cc.; Kuhn, 74-5.]

V.b. *Bird and Fisherman.*

A bird saw a fisherman drawing a fish to land, and pounced down upon it and swallowed it. But soon the fish-hook caught in its throat, and the fisherman began to pull it in. With difficulty the bird freed itself; but henceforth it dared not swallow any fish, for fear of a similar danger, and thus died of hunger.

[Only in Heb. ix., but probably in original, since certainly Indian. (Cf. *Hipotad.*, iv. 101; Benfey, *Pants*, i. 227.)]

V.c. *The Sower.*

When the sower sows his seed some falls on the highway, where the passengers tread it under foot. Others are blown away by the wind. Others picked up by the birds. Some seeds fall on rocky ground, and grow only till the roots reach the rock. Others fall among the thistles. Only a small portion falls in rich earth, where it grows and brings forth fruit. The sower is the Sage; the seed is his wisdom. The seeds that fall by the wayside, &c., are pieces of wisdom that come into one ear only to go out of the other. Those falling on rocky ground are not taken to heart. Those among thorns meet

APPENDIX

with opposition from the senses. Only that which takes root in the heart brings forth fruit in the character.

[*Occurrences in Barlaam.*—In Arab., Georg., and Heb. c. x., and Gr.; probably, therefore, in the original in some form, but the details are from the New Testament.

Source.—*Parable of Sower,* Matt. xiii. 3; Mark iv. 3; Luke viii. 5.

Parallel.—*Sutta Nihata,* tr. Fausböll, pp. 1-5. (Cf. Carus, *Gospel of Buddha,* § 74.)]

VI.a. *The Man in the Well.*
Z. viii., L. p. 93.

A man saw a raging unicorn, and flying from him fell into a pit. But as he fell he caught hold of a branch which saved him from falling to the bottom, while he rested his feet upon a projecting stone. Looking about him he saw two mice, one white and one black, gnawing at the root of the branch which he was holding, while at the bottom of the well he saw a fiery dragon, and near the stone on which his feet rested, a serpent, with four heads. But just at this moment he noticed on the branch he was holding a few drops of honey trickling down, and forgetting the unicorn, the dragon, the snakes, and the mice, he directed his whole thoughts how he might obtain the sweet honey.

Now the unicorn is death, the well is the world, full of manifold evil, the two mice are the night and the day which eat away the branch of life, while the four serpents are the four elements of man's body, and the fiery dragon represents hell. The few drops of honey, the pleasures of this world.

[*Occurrences in Barlaam.*—In Arab., Georg., and Gr., therefore in Indian original.

Indian Original.—Mahabharata, xi. (Cf. Clouston, *Athenæum*, Feb. 7, 1891.) Jaina version, Chinese version, *Avadanas*, i. 132 *seq.*, 191 *seq.*, Tibetan version. (Cf. *Germania*, xxxv. 351 *seq.*) For variations, see *supra*, p. lxxiii.

Parallels.—For symbol of tree, cf. Madhusudana on *Bhagavadgita*, xv. 1. A reference to elephant in *Upanishads*, S.B.E., xv. 167. For resemblance with Yggdrasil, see Grimm, *Teut. Myth.*, 1331, 1536.

Derivates.—Occurs in Bidpai literature, cf. *Bidpai*, ed. Jacobs, p. lxx. (add. *Directorium*, ed. Derenbourg, p. 34 and refs. in note), as well as in almost all versions of *Barlaam*. In Arab. Romance of Avicenna, cf. Noldeke, *Doctor und Garkoch*, p. 53; Berachyah Nakdan, 68 (cf. Steinschneider, Z.D.M.G., xxvii. 562; *Central-Anzeiger*, i. 134; *Uebersetzungen*, 880). *Gesta*, ed. Oesterley, 168; *Legenda aurea*, c. 180; Vincent Bellovac, *Hist.*, xiv. 15; *Mor.*, I., i. 20; Odo de Sherington, *ap.* Hervieux, *Fab. Lat.*, ii. 626; *Abund. Exempl.*, f. 51; Bareleta, *Sermones*, ed. 1505, f. 9; *Spec. Exempl.*, ed. 1487, iv. 16; *Magn. Spec. Exempl.*, ed. Major, s.v. "Delitiæ," iv.; *Libro de los Gatos*, 48; Jacques de Vitry, *Exempla*, ed. Crane, 134; Bozon, *Contes Moralisés*, 29; *Dit de l'Unicorne et du Serpent* in Jubinal, *Nouv. rec.*, ii. 113; and Lidforss, *Choix*, 1877, No. 16; Stephen de Borbone, Hubert de Roman, 50; *Rev. d. lang. rom.*, 3rd ser., ix. 161. Cats Dutch poem, MS.; Manul Philes, *Carmina*, i. 126 *seq.*; Slav. version by Veselovsky (see Kuhn, 77). Chinese Chapbook, *ap.* R.A.S., China branch, XIX., i. 94.

Illustrations.—Schnaase, *Gesch. d. Bild. Kunste*, 2te, Auf., vii. 262, R.A.S., *ut supra;* Philes and Chinese Chapbook, *ut supra; Bidpai*, ed. Jacobs, pp. xxx. 61.

Literature.—Kuhn in *Festgruss an Otto von Bohtingk*, pp. 68-76, with addenda in *Barlaam*, 76-7; Oesterley, Crane, *ut supra;* Toulmin Smith and Meyer on Bozon, p. 239 *seq.*; Landau, *Quellen*, 222 *seq.*; Clouston, *ut supra;* Knust in *Jahrb. rom. eng. Litt.*, vi. 36 *seq.*; *Gott. Gel. Anz.*, 1867, p. 1299 *seq.*; Benfey, *Pants*, i. 81, ii. 528; Jacobs, *ut supra.*]

VI.b. *The Three Friends.*

Z. ix., L. p. 95, C. 438.

A man once had three friends, two of whom he loaded with gifts and friendly acts; the third he neglected. One day he was seized and brought before the King, who ordered him to find security for a great sum. He went to his first friend, who told him he could only give him a single garment. And the second said he would accompany him a little way to the King, but then had to return to his own house. As a last resort he went to the third friend, and begged him to forgive his negligence and help him in his strait. But the third friend received him kindly, and said he would go before to the King and try and rescue him out of the hands of his enemies.

The first friend is wealth; the second, wife and children; the third, good works.

[*Occurrences in Barlaam.*—In Arab., Georg., and Gr. (Z. ix., L. p. 95), therefore in the original.

Indian Original.—Not yet discovered, though Kuhn,

p. 78, gives several Indian proverbs in which good works are called the only friends that accompany you into the next life.

Parallels.—Petrus Alfonsi, *Disc. cler.*, ii., for derivates of which see Goedeke, *Every Man*, 1-7. Cf. Caxton, *Æsop*, ed. Jacobs, Alf. i., A. i. 263-4; *Pirke Eleazar*, 43. (Cf. I. Levi in *Rev. d. Etudes juives*, xviii. 83-9; Steinschneider, *Uebersetzungen*, 864.)

Derivates.—In all translations of *Barlaam;* Rudolf von Ems, *Barlaam*, ed. Pfeiffer, 120-7; *Legenda aurea*, 180; Vincent Bellovac, *Hist.*, xv. 16; *Mor.*, I., iv. 19; III., x. 21; Holkot, *Moralit.*, 28; Bromyard, *Summa*, A. xxi. 5; Junior, *Scala seli*, 9; Nic. Purg., *Dial. creat.*, *Directorium*, iv. 2, D.; Bareleta, *Sermones*, 49; Martin Polon, *Promptuarium*, xi. B.; *Specul. Exempl.*, iv. 17; Wright, *Latin Stories*, 108; *Selentroist*, 15, B.; Bodmer, *Fab.*, 247; H. Sachs., I., i. 100; Herder, *Werke*, ix. 64, ed. 1829; *Svenskt Legendarium*, 615; Jacques de Vitry, *Exempla*, 120; Peregrinus, *Sermones*, f. 30; *Libro de Enxemplos*, No. 16; *Gesta Romanorum*, ed. Oesterley, 138; *Acerra philol.*, 1708, v. 95; Sancho, *Castigos*, 36; Manuel, *Conde Lucanor*, 48.

Dramatic Versions.—*Every Man*, ed. Goedeke, 1865; Peter Vandiest, ed. Logeman, 1893; Christian Ischyrius, *Homulus;* Jaspar Gennep, *Commedia homuli Ein schön Spyl.*, 1540, &c.; *Homulus Comedie ofte spel*, Amsterdam, 1633; G. Lankveld (Macropedius), *Hecastus*, Colon, 1539; L. Rappolt, *Ein schön christlish Spiel, Hecastus, genannt.*; Hans Sachs, *Ein Comedi von dem reichem sterbendem Menschen*, 1649; other German translations by Spanengburg, Ravenstock, Schreckenberger, Saurius, Himmelreich, Striceris *De dudesche Schlomer*, Lubeck, 1584.

Literature.—Goedeke, *Every Man, Homulus und Hekastus, Ein Beitrag zur internationalen Litteraturgeschichte*; Logeman, Levi, Steinschneider, Oesterley, Crane, *ut supra.*]

VI.c. *The King of the Year.*
Z. x., L. p. 98, C. 441.

It was the custom in a certain country to select a stranger to rule over them each year, who for that time had full power and enjoyed all the treasures of the kingdom, but at the end of the year he was stript of all his wealth and power and banished to a desolate island. But on one occasion the King of the year learnt his future fate, and in anticipation sent to the island a large amount of treasure, clothing, food, and all necessities and luxuries, so that he wanted for nothing when the time came for his banishment.

[*Occurrences in Barlaam.*—In Arab., Georg., Heb., and Gr. (Z. x., L. p. 98), therefore in original.

Parallels.—Talmud, *Baba Bathra*, 11b; *Dhammapada*, 25, 235-8; Matt. vi. 19, 20.

Derivates.—Bechai ibn Pakuda, *Choboth Halebaboth* (in Arab., ed. Zotenberg, p. 90); Jacques de Vitry, *Exempla*, ix.; *Legenda aurea*, 180; Stephen de Borbone, *Hubert de Roman*; Vincent Bellovac, *Hist.*, xv. 17; *Mor.*, II., i. 4; Junior, *Scala celi*, 21b.; Bromyard, *Summa*, O., i. 4; *Specul. Exempl.*, iv. 18; Manuel, *Conde Lucanor*, 49; *Libro de Enxemplos*, 310; *Svenskt Legendar.*, 616; Peregrinus, *Sermones*, ix., post Pent.; Paratus, *Sermones*, ii.; *Magn. Specul. Exempl.* s.v. "Mundus;" *Gesta*, ed. Oesterley; Gallensis, *Communialoquium*, VII., i. 5; *Selentroist*, f. 14; Brit. Mus. MS., Add. 26,770, f. 78; 11,284, f. 78; Langbein, *Werke*, vii. 216-9.

Literature.—Oesterley, Crane, Goedeke, 205; Weisslovits, 154-60; Kuhn, 79, 80; Köhler, *Jahrb. Rom. Eng. Litt.*, ii. 22; Cassel, *Aus Litteratur und Symbolik*, 177.]

VI.d. *Dogs and Carrion.*

Dogs are quarrelling about some carrion, when a stranger passes by. They immediately turn upon him and attack him altogether, though he has no desire to interfere with their prey.

The carrion is riches, the dogs worldly people, and the stranger the pious hermit.

> [*Occurrences in Barlaam.*—Only found in Heb., c. xxiii., and Arab., in all three forms of it. (Cf. Rehatsek, p. 140.)]

VI.e. *The Cannibal King.*

A king is forced to flee with wife and children before the enemy. One of the children dies, and they are forced to eat him. So the pious eat from necessity, while others eat with appetite.

> [*Occurrences in Barlaam.*—In Heb. c. xii., and Arab. (cf. Reh., p. 149), not in Gr., which probably omitted it for æsthetic reasons.
> *Indian Original.*—Tibetan, *Dsanglun*, tr. Schmidt, xxviii. seq., ap. Benfey, *Pants,* i. 391.
> *Literature.*—Kuhn, 21 ; Cassel, 227 ; Weisslovits, 87 ; Benfey, *l.c.*]

VI.f. *The Sun of Wisdom.*

Wisdom is like the sun, which shines everywhere and upon all. Yet we cannot always see it, because some have weak sight, and cannot bear its brilliance; others are blind, and cannot see at all.

> [*Occurrences in Barlaam.*—In Heb., c. xv., and Arab. ; only slight traces in Gr.
> *Literature.*—Kuhn, 21 ; Weisslovits, 94.]

VI.g. *The King and Shepherd.*

A king hunting invites a shepherd to eat with him in the heat of the day.

Shepherd. "I cannot eat with thee, for I have already promised another greater than thee."

King. "Who is that?"

Shepherd. "God, who has invited me to fast."

King. "But why fast on such a hot day?"

Shepherd. "I fast for a day still hotter than this."

King. "Eat to-day, fast to-morrow."

Shepherd. "Yes, if you will guarantee that I shall see to-morrow."

[*Occurrences in Barlaam.*—Only in Heb., c. xvi., probably from Mahomedan source.
Literature.—Weisslovits, 97, 101.]

VI.h. *The Bird and the Prophet.*

A bird, fearing for the safety of its eggs, placed them in the nests of other birds. When the storm arose and the waves approached, it went to the various nests and uttered its cry. Its young ones recognised it and flew away with it, while the other fledglings remained to be destroyed.

So a prophet summons the faithful, who alone are saved from destruction by recognising his voice.

[*Occurrences in Barlaam.*—In Heb., c. xix., and Arab.
Literature.—Weisslovits, 109.]

VII.a. *The Heathen King and the Believing Vizier.*

Z. xi., L. p. 113, C. 442.

There was once a king good in everything, except that he was wanting in faith. His vizier desired to cure him of his disbelief, and one night went out with him into the city. Seeing a light in a hut, they looked through and saw a poor couple, clothed in rags, but enjoying themselves with dancing and singing. Then the King asked, "How is it that you and I, so rich in honour and wealth, have never enjoyed so much pleasure as these fools?"

"Why, what do you think of their life, O King?" answered the vizier.

"More wretched, unhappy, and horrid than any I have ever seen," answered the King.

"Then," said the Vizier, "Know, O King, this our life, even of us more fortunately placed of men, seems but as their life in the eyes of the Most High. Only those who seek imperishable wealth are truly happy. And that wealth is, belief in our Lord and Saviour."

[*Occurrences in Barlaam.*—In Arab., Georg., Heb., and Gr. (Z. xi., L. p. 113).

Indian Original.—Unknown, but the happy pair seem to belong to the caste of *Mehter* (cf. Rehatsek, p. 145, *l.c.*; Kuhn, 22 *n.*).

Derivates.—Jacques de Vitry, *Exempla*, ed. Crane, 78; Wright, *Latin Stories*, 4; *Libro de Enxemplos*, 288; Suchomlinoff, *Cyrill of Turoff* (Russ, 1858), pp. 50-3 (cf. Kuhn, 74 *n.*).]

VII.a. i. *The Swimmer*.

A swimmer and his friend went bathing together. The friend got out of his depth, and the swimmer feared that he would drown, but as he went to his assistance, he had the further fear that his friend would seize him and cause them both to drown. But nevertheless he went near, and by inducing his friend to make the appropriate motions saved them both.

[In Arabic only, Reh. 147.]

VII.b. *The Rich Young Man and the Beggar's Daughter*.

Z. xii., L. p. 117, C. 444.

A rich merchant once desired to betroth his son to a wealthy, beautiful, and well-born girl. He, however, refused the match, and fled from his father's house. During his journey he entered a poor man's hut to shelter himself from the heat. There he saw the daughter of the house working with her hands and praising God for His goodness. Asking her why she was so grateful, she replied—"Because the good God has given me the chance of entering Paradise." Struck by this answer, the young man desires to marry her, but her father would not consent till the young man agreed to put aside his rich clothing and live their life. He does so, and for a time assists in the work of the house, till at last the father is convinced of his sincerity and betroths him to his daughter, and then shows him a hidden treasure which he gives to him.

[*Occurrences in Barlaam.*—In Arab., Georg., Heb., and Gr. (Z. xii., L. p. 113), therefore in original. The Halle MS. of the Arab. omits.
Parallels.—Cf. Percy Ballads, *King Cophetua.*]

VII.b. ii. *Education by Love.*

A king had a son who grew up coarse and thoughtless, ill-bred, and undignified. All the learned men of the kingdom tried in vain to improve him. One day his teacher appeared before the King and announced a new misfortune, the Prince had fallen in love. When the King heard this he gave his mantle to the teacher, and thanked him for the good news. Summoning the girl to him, he instructed her to refuse to have anything to do with the Prince till he behaved in a more dignified and well-bred manner. Accordingly the Prince set himself to improve his manners, and soon became a model of propriety.

[*Occurrences in Barlaam.*—Only in Heb., c. xviii., where it is inserted in VII.b.
Parallel.—Boccaccio, *Dec.*, V. i.; Dryden, *Cimon and Iphigenia* (cf. Steele, "To love her was a liberal education").
Literature.—Weisslovits, 108; Kuhn, 43; Landau, *Quellen*, 103.]

VII.c. *Man and Bird.*

Z. vii., L. p 83, C. 435.

A man caught a nightingale, which promised him three precious pieces of advice if he would let him free. He agreed; whereupon the nightingale said, "Do not attempt the impossible. Regret nothing that is past. Believe no improbable tale." The man then let the nightingale free. He, desiring to test him, cried, "Fool, you little know what treasure you have lost. I have within me a pearl as large as an eagle's egg." The man, full of greed, tried to entice the nightingale within his door again, promising to let her go free. The nightingale said, "Now I see what use you will make of my three pieces of advice. I told you never to regret what was past, and yet you are sorry that you let me go free. I advised you not to try the impossible, and yet you are attempting to get me again within your power. I told you never to trust the improbable tale, and yet you believed me when I said that I had within me a pearl greater than my whole body."

[*Occurrences in Barlaam.*—In Arab., Georg., Heb., and Gr., therefore in original.

Indian Original.—Cf. Benfey, *Pants,* i. 380.

Parallels.—*Tutinameh,* tr. Iken, vii. 46; tr. Rosen, i. 137 (cf. Benfey, *l.c.*).

Derivates.—Petrus Alfonsi, *Disc. cler.* xxiii.; Caxton's *Æsop,* ed. Jacobs, Alf. vi.; *Gesta,* ed. Oesterley, 167; Jacques de Vitry, 28; Nic. Purg., *Dial. creat.* 100; Vartan, *Fables,* xiii.; Bromyard, *Summa,* M. xi. 78; Junior, *Scala celi,* vii.b.; Wright, *Latin Stories,*

b. 170; *Legenda aurea*, ed. Grässe, 180; *Libro de Enxemplos*, 53; Stainhöwel, *Æsop*, collect. vi. (and derivates); Le Grand, *Fabliaux*, iii. 113; *Mystère du roi Advenis* in *Hist. du théatre franc.*, ii. 475; *Marie de France*, ed. Roquefort, i. 314, ii. 324; *Selentroist*, 14.b; Luther, *Tischreden*, 612; Hans Sachs, D. iv. 428; Kirchhof, *Wendunmuth*, iv. 34; Wieland, *Vogelgesang*, ap. *Werke*, ed. 1796, xviii. 315; *Le lai de Loiselet*, ed. G. Paris, 1883; Lydgate, *Chorle and Byrde*; cf. *Temple of Glass*, edit. Schick, p. c. 135.

Literature.—Oesterley, Crane, Benfey, Jacobs, Paris, Schick, *ll.cc.*]

VII.c. ii. *The Tyrannical King.*

There was once a king who made every one tremble around him. One day a servant, when handing him the soup, from fear spilt a little. Before the King could express his rage, the servant emptied the whole tureen. "Why did you do that?" said the King. "I knew, my Lord," said the servant, "that you would punish me severely for my first small fault, and thereby lose dignity in the eyes of your people, so I therefore arranged to do something worth the punishment I saw forthcoming." Thereupon the King forgave him, and became less tyrannical in future.

[*Occurrences in Barlaam.*—Only in Heb., c. xxiv.]

VII.d. *Desert and Garden.*

There is a desert full of robbers and beasts of prey. In the midst is a garden with a wall too high to be scaled; on the other side is a sea of poison, over which blows a fiery simoon.

The desert is the world, the garden represents the joys of the faithful, the sea the misery of the wicked.

[*Occurrences in Barlaam.*—In Arabic, Reh., 151.]

VII.e. *Language of Animals.*

A man once learnt the language of animals, but on condition that if he betrayed the secret he would have to die. One night he heard an ass recommend an ox to feign illness so as to escape work, whereat he laughed aloud. His wife wished to know why he laughed, but he would not tell her. Next day, when the ox pretended to be ill he ordered the ass to do its work; and at night, when the ass returned, he told the ox that he was to be slain on the morrow if he were not better. Whereat the man laughed again. His wife was eager to know why he laughed, even though he told her it would be his death to let her know. "Either your death or mine," said the wife, "for I will not eat till I know;" so the man agreed to let her know the next day, and prepared for his death. All was sadness in the house, even the dogs would not eat their food, but a cock and his wives pecked away merrily, till one of the dogs said, "Do you not know our master is to die to-day?" "More fool he," said the cock; "I can rule ten wives." "What can you do?" said the dog. "Take a stick to her," said the cock, "and I'll warrant she won't want to know his secrets." The man, who had heard this, followed the cock's advice, and saved his life.

[*Occurrences in Barlaam.*—Only in Heb., c. xxiv., where the language is taught by King Solomon, but certainly Indian in origin.

Indian Original.—*Harivanso*, 1274 *seq.* (tr. Benfey, *Or. u. Oec.*, ii. 148); *Ramayana*, II., xxxv. 15 *seq.*; Tamel, *Vedala Cadai* (tr. Rabington, *Misc. Trans.*, i. 55).

Parallels.—*Æsop*, ed. Halm, 18 (cf. Fraser, *Arch. Rev.*, i. 81-91, 161-181).

Derivates.—*Tutinameh*, tr. Rosen., ii. 236; Peter Alfonsi, *Disc. cler.*, ii. 7; *Arabian Nights*, First tale in all versions; *Gesta Romanorum*, ed. Oesterley, qy. Wuk, *Volk's Märchen der Serben*, iii. (Denton, *Serbian Folk-tales;* Leger, *Contes Slaves*, xi.; Krauss, *Sagen der Süd Slaven*, I. xcvii.); *Nonthu Kpakaranam* in *Zeits. f. Ethn.*, i. 152; Morlini, *Novellæ*, lxxi.; Straparola, xii. 3; Landes, *Contes Annamites*, xcix.; Radloof, *Proben*, vi. 250 *seq.* (man dies); Schreck, *Finn. Märchen;* Koelle, *Afric. Nat. Lit.* (Grimm, Hunt, ii. 541); Raymond Lully, *Libre de Maravelles*, VII., vi. 42; Reinisch, *Sahosprache*, i. 109 *seq.*

Literature.—Benfey, *Märchen von der Tiersprache* in *Orient und Occident*, ii. 133-71 (add. *Klein Schrift*, ii. 234-6); J. G. Fraser, *Language of Animals*, *ut supra;* Steinschneider, *Manna*, 101 *seq.*; *Arch. Slav. Phil.*, vii. 318, 515; *Z.D.M.G.*, xlvi. 402; Kuhn, 81.]

VII.f. *The Robbers' Nemesis.*

Two swindlers plotted to rob a stranger merchant of his money. They brought him jewels to a feast, but intended to rob him of them; but each envying the other his share in the booty, secretly put poison in his food, so they both died, and the merchant was saved.

> [*Occurrences in Barlaam.*—Only in Heb., c. 27, but certainly Indian.
> *Indian Original.*—*Vedabbha Jataka,* ed. Cowell, No. 48, i. 121-4, Kashmir version, tr. Knowles, in *Orientalist,* i. 52-60.
> *Parallels.*—Cosquin, *Contes de Lorraine,* No. xxx. (Cf. notes i. 287-8.)
> *Derivates.* — Persian, Attar, *Macibat Nama,* tr. Ruckart, Z.D.M.G., xiv. 280-7 (tr. Warner, *Prov. Pers. Cent.*, Leyden, 1644, p. 31); *Arabian Nights,* tr. Burton, ii. 158 *seq.*, and supp., i. 250 seq. (cf. *Orientalist,* i. 46-7); Tibetan Schiefner-Ralston, 286-7; Chaucer, *Pardonere's Tale; Ciento Novelle Antiche,* lxxxiii. (libro di novelle, lxxxii.); Morlini, *Novellæ,* xlii.; D'Ancona, *Rappres Sacre,* ii. 33 *seq.*; Fabricius, *Cod. Apoc. Nov. Test.*, iii. 395; Robles, *Leyendas Moriscas,* No. 1; Hans Sachs Braga, *Contos,* No. 143; P. Paris, *Man. Franc.*, iv. 83; L. Hunt, *Death and the Ruffians.*
> *Literature.*—H. D. Francis, *Vedabbha Jataka compared with the Pardonere's Tale,* Camb., 1884, 8vo, pp. 12; R. Morris, *Cont. Rev.*, 1881, i. 738; *Academy,* 22nd Dec. 1883, 12th Jan. 1884; Tawney in *Jour. Phil.*, 212-8: Clouston, *Pop. Tales,* i. 379-406; Chaucer Society, *Originals,* 129-34, 415-36; Skeat, *Chaucer,* iii. 439-45; Grünbaum, *Neue Beiträge,* 279-82; Kuhn, 82.]

IX.a. *The Tame Gazelle.*

Z. xiii., L., p. 130, C. 446.

A rich man had once a young gazelle. As it grew up it began to long for the wilderness. So one day it went and joined a herd of wild gazelles, but came back at night. And henceforth it used to join the herd every day. This at last was noticed. And the servants of the rich man followed it on horseback, killed many of the wild gazelles, and drove back the tame one, which they ever afterwards kept chained up.

[*Occurrences in Barlaam.*—In Arab., Georg., and Gr. (Z. xiii., L. p. 130, C. 446). Not in Hebrew, which substitutes "Greedy Hound," ix.b. *q.v.*]

IX.b. *The Greedy Dog.*

In two neighbouring cities a marriage was to be held on one and the same day. A greedy dog who knew of this determined to attend both wedding breakfasts. He set off early for one town, but arrived too late, and when he went to the other the feasting was over, and he only got blows.

[*Occurrences in Barlaam.*—Only in Heb., c. xvii., where it is substituted for "The Tame Gazelle."
Parallels.—Æsop, *Dog and Shadow* (Caxton, ed. Jacobs, Ro. i. 5).]

X.a. *The Two Halves of a King's Life.*

A prince being born during the conjunction of Jupiter and Venus, astrologers prophesy a change in his life. When he succeeds he lives in great splendour till middle age. At a great feast, surrounded by his most costly ornaments, he thinks of looking at himself in the glass, and sees his grey hairs, which cause him to devote himself to a life of piety.

> [*Occurrences in Barlaam.*—Only one of the Arab. versions.
>
> *Indian Original.*—Clearly a variant of the life of Buddha, wherefore Kuhn suggests derived from the *Kitab-al-Budd.*
>
> *Literature.*—Hommel, *l.c.* 166; Kuhn, 15.

X.b. *King, Man, and Skull.*

A wicked king was bringing his realm to ruin, when a sage came before him and kicked a skull in front of him. Then he took weights and scales and measured out as much dust as would weigh a dihrem, and placed this in the eyes of the skull. On being asked what was the meaning of this action, he said, "This skull was the skull of a king, and he used to pay royal honours to it; but finding it insensible, he then kicked it about to see if it could feel contumely. But as the King had seen, there was no sign of resentment in the skull; and he wanted to know if that could be a king's skull when a dihrem weight of dust could cover the eyes, which, when living, possessed all they saw." The King was struck by the worthlessness of all his possessions, and became converted to piety.

> [*Occurrences in Barlaam.*—Only in one of Arab. versions and in its Persian translation. Probably derived from Alexander Romance.
>
> *Parallels.*—Talmud, *Tamid*, 52*b* (Steinschneider *Uebers.*, 896).
>
> *Literature.*—Hommel, 167 *l.c.*; Zacher, *Alex. Magni Iter*, 1859, p. 17; Hertz, *Aristoteles in Alexander*

Dichtungen; Eisenmenger, *Entdecktes Judenthum,* ii. 321; Vogelstein, *Adnotationes ad Fabulas de Alex. Magno,* 1865, p. 16; Steinschneider, *l. c.*, § 540.

X.c. *The Prince who left his Father's House.*

A prince, the only son of a king, in the midst of play in his boyhood, took one step and said, "Your fate is to have trouble." Then a second step, and said, "And to become old and feeble." Then a third step, saying, "And then you will die." Astrologers, thereupon, announced that he would become a great saint. And the King put him a guard so he could never be left alone. One day, however, he escapes them, and encounters a funeral, and learns that all men must die. He tells his guard that if this is true they are mad. The astrologers recommend the King to marry the Prince. On the wedding night, the Prince calls for wine for his bride, and when she sleeps rises and leaves her. He finds a companion, and they both take refuge in the castle of another king, where the Princess falls in love with the Prince; but he rejects her overtures and flees. The King has him pursued and brought back. He tells the following parables:—

The Drunken King's Son who fell into a Grave.
The Thieves who stole a Golden Vessel containing Serpents.
The Prince freed from Prison falling into a Pit with Dragons.
The Man who fell among the Ghouls.

By these parables he frees himself, and wanders about converting numbers to the true faith, till at last he comes back to his father, the old King.

> [*Occurrences in Barlaam.*—Only in Bombay form of the Arab. version.
> *Indian Original.*—Clearly a variant of the Buddha legend.
> *Parallels.*—The legend of St. Alexis has the episode of the desertion of the wife on the wedding night.
> *Literature.*—Hommel, 169-72; Kuhn, 15.]

X.c. iv. *The Man among the Ghouls.*

A ship was shipwrecked on an island inhabited by ghouls, who turned themselves into beautiful maidens to entice the shipwrecked sailors. They lived very happily for some time, till the captain came across an earlier victim of the ghouls, who told him what they were. He also told him that their only chance of escape was from a gigantic bird who visited the island once a year. But the captain is warned, that if he looks back when escaping, he will fall off and be drowned. On the appointed day the sailors intoxicate the ghouls, and perch upon the back of the bird. The ghouls, however, call to the sailors as they depart, and when the captain lands he finds that none of the sailors have survived the voyage.

> [*Occurrences in Barlaam.*—Only in one form of Arab.
> *Indian Original.*—*Valahassa Jataka,* ed. Fausböll, ii. 127; tr. E. Müller in *Pali Grammar,* 128 *seq.*
> *Parallels.*—*Myth Sirens* (cf. *Academy,* 13, 27th Aug.

1881); *Sindabad Cycle* (Clouston, 50, 150, 235), tr. Tawney, i. 60, *Katha-Sarit-Sagara*.

Derivates of Indian.—*Divya Vadana*, ed. Cowell and Neil, 524-6; Tibetan in J.R.A.S., 1888, 504-6; Chinese, Beal, *Romantic Legend*, 332-40; *Buddhist Records*, ii. 241.

Literature.—H. Wenzel, *A Jataka Tale from Tibetan* in J.R.A.S., *l.c.*; Kuhn, 81; Hommel, 172.]

XII.a. *The Amorous Wife.*

A young man, having married a wife of a passionate temperament, told her whenever she could not restrain her feelings to let down her hair as a signal. It happened that a war broke out, and the young man was summoned to join the army. But just as he was leaving, his wife let down her hair, and the battle was won without him. When he was remonstrated with, he replied, "I had an enemy at home with whom I had to fight."

[*Occurrences in Barlaam.*—Only in Georg. version, in the conversation between Theudas and the King.
Literature.—Hommel in Weisslovitz, 148.]

XIII.a. *The Youth who had never seen a Woman.*

Z. xiv., L. p. 220, C. 446.

A king had a son born to him in his old age, and was warned by his astrologers and physicians that his son would be blind if he ever saw the light before he was twelve years old. Accordingly the King built for him a subterranean chamber, where he was kept till he was past the fatal age. Thereupon he was taken out from his retreat and shown all the beauties of the world, gold and jewels, and arms, and carriages and horses, and beautiful dresses. But seeing some women pass he asked what they might be, and was told, "Demons, who lead men astray." Afterwards the King asked him which of all the beautiful things he had seen he desired most; and the Prince answered, "The demons which lead men astray."

>[*Occurrences in Barlaam.*—In Georg. and Gr. (Z. xiv., L. p. 220), but only in Bombay version of the Arab. text and not at all in Heb., yet clearly in original (see next section).
>
>*Indian Original.*—Story of Rshyasrnga in *Mahabharata*, iii. 9999; and *Ramayana*, I. ix. (cf. Schiefner in *Mel. Asiat.*, viii. 112-6).
>
>*Derivates.*—R. Basset, *Vie d'Abba Yohanni*, Texte éthiopien, trad. franc., Algiers, 1884 (not from Ethiopic Barlaam); Jacques de Vitry, *Exempla*, 82; Wright, *Latin Stories*, 3, cf. 78; *Libro de Enxemplos*, 231; *Scala celi*, f. 15.b.; *Prompt. Exempl.* L. xxiv.; Boccaccio, *Decameron*, Day IV.; Zambrini, *Libro di Novelle*.
>
>*Literature.*—Crane, *l.c.*; Landau, *Quellen*, 223; D'Ancona, *Studj*, 307; Kuhn, 80.]

XIII.b. *Peacock and Raven.*

A king showed a foreign merchant his treasures, and asked him if there were anything wanting. The merchant said, "Only a peacock," which he described. So the King sent his vizier with a large amount of gold to buy a peacock. But he hid the gold, and dyed a raven, and brought it to the King. But shortly afterwards the merchant brought two real peacocks as a present to the King. The vizier maintained that his was the authentic bird. Whereupon the merchant poured hot water on the raven, which changed colour at once. The same test applied to the peacocks only made them more beautiful. So the King honoured the merchant and punished the vizier.

The merchant is Buddha, the vizier an idolater, the peacock belief in God, the raven heresy.

[*Occurrences in Barlaam.*—Only in Bombay text of Arab., but certainly Indian (see next section).

Indian Original.—Baveru Jataka, tr. Morris in *Folklore Journal*, iii. 124.

Parallel.—Æsop, *Daw in Peacock's Feathers* (cf. Caxton, Ro. ii. 15, and note i. 77 *n*).

Literature.—Kuhn, 31; Jacobs, *l.c.*

The Lyf of Saynt balaam.

A

¶ Here foloweth of Balaam the Hermyte.

BALAAM of whome faynt Johan damafcene made the hyftorye with grete dyligence / In whome deuyne grace fo wroughte that he conuerted to the feythe faynt Jofaphat / & thenne as al ynde was ful of cryften peple & of monkes / ther aroos a puyffaunt kyng wiche was named anemyr whiche made grete perfecucion to criften men & fpecyally to monkes / & it happed fo that one whiche was frende of the kynge & chyef in his paleys / by the Infpiracion of deuyne grace lefte the halle ryal / for to entre in to the ordre of monkes / & whan the kyng herd fay that he was criften he was wode for angre / and dyd fo feche hym thorugh euery deferte til that he was foūde with grete payne / and thenne he was brought tofore hym / & whan he fawe hym in a vyle cote & moche lene for hongre / whyche was wonte to be couerd with precious clothynge and habounded in moche richeffe & fayd to hym o thou fole & out of thy mynde / why haft thou chaunged

chaunged thyn honour in to vylonye / & arte made the player of children / and he said to hym yf thou wylt here of me reson / put fro the thyn enemyes / thenne the kyng demaūded hym who were his enemyes / & he said to hym yre & couetyse / for they empesshe & lette / that trouthe may not be seen / ne to assaye prudence / and equyte To whom the kyng said / lete it be as thou sayest / & that other said / the foles despyse the thynges that ben / lyke as they were not / and he that hath not the taste of the thynges that ben / he shall not vse the swetnesse of them / & may not lerne the trouthe of them that been not / and whan he had shewyd many thynges of the mysterye of thyncarnacion / the kynge sayd to hym yf I had not promysed the atte begynnynge that I shold put aweye yre fro my counceyl I sholde caste thy bodye in to the fyre / Goo thy weye and flee fro myn eyen that I see the nomore / & that I now dystresse the not / and anone the man of god wente his waye al heuyly / by cause he had not suffred marterdom /

Thus thenne in this mene whyle it happyd that the kyng whiche had noo chylde / ther was a fayr sone borne of his wyf / and was callyd Josaphat & the kyng assemblyd a righte grete companye of peple for to make sacrefyse to his goddes for the natyuyte of his sone / & also assemblyd

aſſemblyd lv aſtronomyens / of whom he enquyred what ſhold befalle of his ſone / & they ſayd to hym that he ſhold be grete in power & in richeſſes / & one more wyſe than another ſaid / ſyr this childe that is born ſhal not be in thy reygne / but he ſhal be in another moche better without comparyſon / and know thou that I ſuppoſe that he ſhal be of cryſten relygyon / which thou perſecuteſt / & that ſayd not he of hym ſelf / but he ſayd it by Inſpyracion of god / And whan the kynge herde that he doubted moche and dyd do make without the cyte a ryȝt noble paleys / and therein ſette he hys ſone for to dwell and abyde / and ſette right fayre yongelynges / and commaūded them that they ſhold not ſpeke to hym of deth / ne of old age / ne of ſekenes / ne of pouerte ne of no thynge that may gyue hym cauſe of heuynes but ſay to hym alle thynges that ben ioyous / ſo that hys minde may be eſpryſed with gladnes / & that he thynke on no thynge to come / and anone as ony of his ſervauntes were ſeke / The kynge commaunded for to take hem aweye / and ſette another hool in hys ſtede / and commaunded that no mencyon ſhold be made to hym of Jheſu cryſte / ❧ In that tyme was wyth the kynge a man whych was ſecretely cryſten / and was chyef emonge alle the noble

prynces

prynces of the kynge / and as he wente on a
tyme to hunte wyth the kynge / he fond a
pour man lyeng on the grounde / whiche was
hurte on the foot of a beeſt / whyche prayed
that he wold receyue hym / and that he myght
of hym be holpen by ſomme meane / and the
knyght ſayd I ſhall receyue the gladly / but I
wote not how thou mayſt doo ony prouffyte /
And he ſayd to hym I am a leche of wordes /
& yf ony be hurte by wordes I can wel gyue
hym a medecyne / and the knyght ſette it at
noughte all that he ſayd / but he receyued hym
onely for goddes ſake / and helyd hym and
thenne prynces enuyous and malycyous ſawe
that this prynce was ſoo grete and gracyous
with the kynge accuſed hym to the kynge /
and ſayd that he was not onely torned to the
cryſten feythe / but enforced to withdrawe fro
hym his royame / and that he moeuyd and
ſolycyted the companye and counceylled theym
therto / And yf thou wylt know it ſayd they /
thenne calle hym ſecretelye / and ſay to hym
that this lyf is ſone doon / and therfore thou
wylte leue the glorye of the worlde and of thy
royame and affirme that thou wylt take the
habyte of monkes / whome thou haſt ſoo perſecuted by ygnoraunce / and after thou ſhalt ſee
what he ſhal anſwer and whan the kynge had
doon

doon alle lyke as they had sayd / the knyghte
that knewe noo thyng of the treason beganne
to wepe and prayſed moche the counceyll of
the kynge / and remembryd hym of the vanyte
of the world and counceylled hym to doo it as
ſone as he myght / and whan the kynge herde
hym ſaye ſoo / he ſuppoſed it had been trewe
that the other had ſayd to hym how be it he
ſayd no thynge / & thenne he vnderſtood and
apperceyued that the kyng had taken his wordes
in euyl and wente and tolde al this vnto the
leche of wordes alle by ordre / and he ſayd to
hym / knowe thou for trouthe that the kynge
feryth that thou wylte aſſaylle his royame /
aryſe thou to morowe / and ſhaue of thyn heer
and doo of thy veſtements / and clothe the in
hayr in manere of a monke / and goo erlye to
the kynge / whan he ſhall demaunde the what
thou meneſt / thou ſhalt anſwer / my lord kyng
I am redy to follow the / For yf the waye by
whyche thou deſyreſt to goo be harde yf I be
with the it ſhal be the lyghter to the / and lyke
as thou haſt had me in proſperyte / ſo ſhalt
thou have me in aduerſyte / I am al redy /
wherfore taryeſt thou / and whan he had thys
doon and ſayd by ordre / the kynge was abaſſhed
& repreuyd the falſe men / and dyd to hym
more honoure thenne he dyd before / and after
thys

thys the kynges fone that was nouryffhed in the paleys came to age and grewe and was playnely taught in al wyfdom / and he meruaylled wherfore hys fader had fo enclofed hym / and called one of hys feruauntes whiche was more famylyer wyth hym fecretely / & demaunded hym of this thynge / and fayd to hym that he was in grete heuyneffe that he myght not goo oute / And that his mete ne drynke fauerid hym not ne dyd hym no good / and whan hys fader herde this / he was ful of forowe / and anone he lete do make redy horfes and ioyeful felawfhyp to accompanye hym in fuche wyfe that no thynge dyfhonefte fhold happen to hym & on a tyme thus as the kynges fone wente he mette a mefel and a blynde man / and whan he fawe them he was abaffhed / & enquyred what them ayled and his feruauntes fayd thyfe ben paffyons that comen to men / and he demaunded yf the paffyons comen to all men / and they fayd nay / Thenne fayd he ben they knowen which men fhal fuffre thyfe paffyons / without dyffynicion / and they anfwerd who is he that may knowe thaduentures of men / and he begun to be moche anguyffhous for the Incuftomable thynge herof / & another tyme he fonde a man moche aged whiche had his chere frounced / his teth fallen & was al
croked

croked for age / wherof he was abaſſhed and
ſaid he deſyred to knowe the myracle of thys
vyſyon / and whan he knewe that thys was by
cauſe he had lyued many yerys / and thenne he
demaunded what ſhold be the ende / and they
ſayd dethe / and he ſayd / is then the dethe
the ende of alle men or of ſomme and they
ſayd for certeyn that alle men muſt deye / And
whan he knewe that alle ſholde deye / he demaunded them in how many yerys that ſhold
happene / and they ſayd in olde age of four
ſcore yere or an hondred / and after that age
the dethe followeth / and thys yonge man remembryd ofte in hys herte thyſe thynges / and
was in grete dyſcomforte / but he ſhewyd hym
moche glad tofore his fader / and he deſyred
moche to be enformed and taughte in thyſe
thynges /

⁋ And thenne there was a monke of parfyte
lyf and good opynyon that dwellyd in the
deſerte of the londe of Sennaar named balaam /
And thys monke knewe by the holy ghooſt
what was done aboute this kynges ſone / and
toke the abbyte of a marchaunte / and came
vnto the cytee and ſpake to the greteſt go-
uernour of the kynges ſone / and ſayd to hym
I am a marchaunte and haue a precyous ſtone
to ſelle whyche gyueth ſyght to blynde men /
&

& heryng to deef men Hyt maketh the dombe to ſpeke / and gyueth wyſedom to fooles / and therfore brynge me to the kynges ſone and I ſhal delyuer it to hym / To whom he ſayd thou ſeemeſt a man of prudente nature but thy wordes accorde no thynge to wyſedom / Neuertheleſſe yf I had knowleche of that ſtone / ſhewe it me / and yf it be ſuche as thou ſayeſt / and ſo proued / thou ſhalt haue right grete honoures of the kynges ſone / To whome balaam ſayd / my ſtone hath yet ſuche vertue / that he that ſeeth it / and hath none hool ſyght and kepeth not entyer chaſtyte / yf he happelye ſawe it / the vertue vyſyble that he hath he ſhold leſe it / and I that am a phyſycyen ſee wel that thou haſt not thy ſyght hoole / but I vnderſtonde that the kynges ſone is chaſte and hath ryght faire eyen and hoole / And thenne the man ſayd yf it be ſo ſhewe it not to me / For myn eyen ben not hoole / and am foule of ſynne / and balaam ſayd thys thynge apperteyneth to the kynges ſone / and therfore brynge me to hym anone / and he anone tolde this to the kynges ſone / and broughte hym anone in / And he receyued hym honourably / and thenne balaam ſayd to hym / thou haſt doon wel / for thou haſt not taken hede of my lytelneſſe that apperyth withoutforth / but thou haſt doon lyke

vnto

vnto a noble kynge / whyche whan he rood in his chaar cladde wyth clothes of gold and mette wyth poure men whiche were cladde wyth torne clothes / ❧ And anone he fprange out of his chare / and fyl doun to their feet and worfhypped theym / and his barons toke thys euyl / and were aferde to repreue hym therof / but they fayd to hys brother how the kynge had doon thynge ageynft hys ryal mageftie / and hys brother repreuyd hym therof / and the kynge had fuche a cuftome that whan one fhold be delyuerd to deth / the kynge fholde fende hys cryar wyth hys trompe that was ordeyned therto /

And on the euen he fente the cryar wyth the trompe before hys brothers gate / and made to fowne the trompe and whan the kynges brother herde thys / He was in dyfpayr of fauynge of hys lyf / and coude not flepe of all the nyght and made hys teftamente / and on the morne erlye he cladde hym in blacke / and came wepynge wyth his wyf and chyldren to the kynges paleys / and the kynge made hym come tofore hym and fayd to hym / a fool that thou arte / yf thou hafte herde the meffager of thy brother / to whom thou knoweft wel thou haft not trefpaced and doubteft foo moche / How ought not I thenne doubte the meffagers of our lord / ageynft whome I haue foo ofte
fynned /

synned / whyche sygnefyed vnto me more clerely
the dethe thenne the trompe / and shewed to me
horrible comyng of the Juge / & after this he
dyd doo make foure cheftys / and dyd doo couer
two of them with golde without forthe / and dyd
doo fylle them wyth boones of deed men and of
fylthe / And the other two he dyd doo pytche /
And dyd doo fylle theym wyth precyous stones
and ryche gemmys / And after thys the kynge
dyd doo calle his grete barons by caufe he knew
wel that they compleyned of hym to his brother /
and dyd doo fette thyfe foure cheftys tofore
them and demaunded of them which were mofte
precious and they fayd that the two that were
gylte / were mooft of valewe / Thenne the kyng
commaunded that they shold be opened / and
anone a grete stenche yffued out of them and
the kynge fayd they be lyke them that be
clothed wyth precious veftementes / and been
ful wythinforth of ordure and of synne and
after he made opene the other / and there yffued
a meruayllous swete odour / and after the kyng
fayd / thyfe been femblable to the poure men
that I mette and honoured / for though they be
clad of foule veftymens / yet shyne they wythinforth with good odour of good vertues / and ye
take none hede but to that wythoutforthe / and
confydere not what is wythin / and thou haft
doon

doon to me lyke as that kyng dyd / For thou
haft wel receyued me / and after thys balaam
beganne to telle to hym a longe fermone of the
creacyon of the world / and of the Day of Juge-
mente / and of the rewarde of good and euyl /
and began ftrongelye to blame them that worfhyp ydolles / and told to hym of theyr folye
fuch an exaumple as followeth fayeng / That
an archer toke a lytel byrde callyd a nyghtyngale / and whan he wold haue flayne thys
nyghtyngale ther was a voys giuen to the nyghtyngale whyche fayd / O thou man what fhold
it auayle the yf thou flee me / Thou mayfte not
fylle thy bely wyth me / but and yf thou wylt
lete me goo / I fhal teche the thre wyfedomes /
that yf thou kepe them dylygentely / thou
mayft haue grete prouffite thereby / Thenne he
was abaffhed of his wordes / and promyfed that
he wold lete hym goo / yf he wold telle hym
his wyfdomes / Thenne the byrde fayd / ftudye
neuer to take that thynge that thou mayft not
take / & of thynge lofte / whiche may not be
recoueryd / forowe neuer therfore / ne byleue
neuer thynge that is Incredyble / Kepe wel
thyfe thre thynges / and thou fhalte doo wel /
and thenne he lete the byrde goo as he had
promyfed / and thenne the nyghtyngale fleyng
in the ayer fayd to hym / alas thou wretched
                                             man

man thou hafte had euyl counceyl / for thou haft lofte thys day grete trefour / For I haue in my bowellys a precyous margaryte / whyche is gretter than the egge of an oftrych / and he herde that / he was moche wroth and forowed fore by caufe he had leten hir goo / and enforced hym al that he coude to take hyr ageyne fayeng / Come ageyn to my hows / and I fhal fhew to the al humanyte / and gyue to the alle that fhal nede the / and after fhal lete the goo honourably / where as thou wylte Thenne fayd the nyghtyngale to hym Now I knowe wel that thou art a foole / fore thou haft no prouffyte in the wyfedoms that I haue fayd to the / For thou art ryght forowful for me whome thou haft lofte / whyche am Irrecuperable / and yet thou weneft to take me / where thou mayft not come fo hyghe as I am / and furthermore where thou beleueft to be in me a precyous ftone more thenne the egge of an oftrytch / whan alle my body may not atteyne to the gretenefle of fuche an egge / And in lyke wyfe be they foolys that adoure and truft in ydolles / for they worfhyp that whiche they haue made / and calle theym whome they haue made kepars of them / and after he beganne to dyfpute ageynfte the fallace of the world and delite and vanyte therof / and broughte forth many enfaumples and fayd /
They

They that delyte the delytes corporalle / and
fuffre their fowles deye for hungre / ben lyke
to a man that fledde tofore an vnycorn that
he fhold not deuoure hym / and in fleyng / he
fyl in to a grete pytte / and as he fyl he caughte
a braunche of a tre with his hande / and fette
his feet vpon a flydyng place / and thenne two
myfe that one whyte / and that other blacke
whyche wythoute ceffyng gnewe the rote of
the tree /

And had almofte gnawen it a fondre And he
fawe in the bottom of thys pytte an horryble
dragon caftynge fyre and had his mouthe opene
and defyred to deuoure hym / vpon the flydyng
place on which his feet ftood / he fawe the
heedes of foure ferpentes whyche yffueden there /
and thenne he lefte vp his eyen and fawe a lytel
hony that henge in the bowes of the tre / &
forgat the perylle that he was in / and gaue
hym al to the fwetenes of that lytel hony / the
vnycorne is the fygure of deth / which continu-
elly foloweth man / and defyreth to take hym /
The pytte is the world whiche is ful of al
wyckedneffe / the tree is the lyf of euery man /
whiche by the two myfe that ben the day and
nyght & the houres therof Inceffantly been
wafted and approched to the cuttyng or gnaw-
yng a fonder / the place where the iiij ferpentes
where

where is the body ordeyned by the foure elementes / by whiche the ioynture of the membrys is corupte in bodyes dyſhordynate / The orrible dragon is the mouthe of helle whiche deſyreth to deuoure al creatures / The ſwetenes of the hony in the bowes of the tree / is the falſe deceyuable delectacyon of the world by whiche man is deceyued / ſo that he taketh no hede of the perylle that he is in / and yet he ſayd that they that loue the worlde ben ſemblable to a man that had thre frendes / of whiche he loued the fyrſte as moche as hym ſelf / and he louyd the ſecond leſſe thenne hym ſelf / & louyd the thyrd a lytel or nought / and it happed ſo that this man was in grete perylle of his lyf / and was ſomoned tofore the kynge / thenne he ranne to hys fyrſte frende / and demaunded of hym hys helpe / and tolde to hym how he had alweye louyd hym / to whome he ſayde / I haue other frendes with whom I muſt be this day / and I wote not who thou arte / therfore I may not helpe the / yet neuertheleſſe I ſhal gyue to the two ſloppes wyth whyche thou mayſt couer the / and thenne he wente aweye moche ſorowful / and wente to that other frende / and requyred alſo his ayde / and he ſayd to hym I may not attende to goo wyth the to thys debate / for I haue grete charge / but I ſhal yet felau-
ſhyp

shyp the vnto the gate of the paleys / & thenne I shal retorne ageyn and doo myn own nedes / and he beyng heuy and as dispayred wente to the thyrde frende and sayd to hym / I haue noo reson to speke to the / ne I haue not loued the as I oughte / but I am in trybulacion and with-oute frendes / and praye the that thou helpe me / and that other sayd wyth glad chere / certes I confesse to be thy dere frende / and haue not forgoten the lytel benefayte that thou hast doon to me / and I shal goo ryght gladly wyth the tofore the kynge / for to see what shal be de-maunded of the and I shal praye the kynge for the / The fyrst frende is possessyon of richesse For whyche man putteth hym in many perylles / and whan the dethe cometh he hath no more of hit but a cloth for to wynde hym for to be buryed / The second frende is hys sones / hys wyf and kynne / whyche goo wyth hym to hys graue / and anone retorne to entende to theyr owne nedes / The thyrd frende is feythe hope and charyte and other good werkys / Whyche we haue doon / that whan we yssue out of our bodyes / they may wel goo tofore vs and praye god for vs / and they may wel delyuer vs fro the deuylles our enemyes / and yet we sayd accordyng to thys / that in a certayn cyte is a custome / that they of the cite shal chese euery
yere

yere a straūge man and vnknowen for to be theyr prynce / and they shal gyue hym puyssaunce to doo what someuer he wyl / And gouerne the contree wythout ony other constytucion / and he beyng thus in grete delyces / and wenyng euer to contynue / sodeynlye they of the cytee shold aryse ageynste hym / and lede hym naked thorugh the cyte / & after sende hym in to an yle in exyle /

And there he shold fynde neyther mete ne clothe / but shold be constreyned to be peryshed for hungre and colde /

And after that they wolde enhaunce another to the kyngdome / and thus they dyd longe / At the laste they took one whyche knewe theyr custome And he sente tofore hym in to that yle grete tresoure wythoute nombre duryng alle hys yere /

And whan his yere was accomplysshed and passed / he was put out and put to exyle lyke the other / and where as the other that had ben tofore hym peryshed for colde and hongre / he habounded in grete rychesses & delyces / and this cyte is the world / and the cytezeyns ben the prynces of derkenesse / whiche fede vs with false delectacyon of the world / and thenne the deth cometh whan we take none hede / and that we ben sente in exyle to the
place

place of derkeneffe / and the rycheffes that ben
tofore fente / ben don by the handes of poure
men / and whan balaam had parfytely taughte
the kynges fone / & wold leue his fader for to
folowe hym balaam faid to hym yf thou wylte
doo thus thou fhalt be femblable to a yonge
man / that whan he fhold haue weddyd a noble
wyf / he forfoke hyr and fledde aweye / and
came in to a place where as he fawe a virgyn
doughter of an olde poure man that laboured /
and preyfed god with hir mowthe / To whome
he fayd what is that thou doeft doughter that
arte fo poure & alweye thou thankeft god like
as thou haddeft receyued grete thynges of hym /

To whome fhe fayd / lyke as a lytel medecyne
ofte delyuereth a grete langour and payne /
right fo for to gyue to god thankynges alweye
of a lytell yefte / is made a gyuer of grete yeftes
for the thynges that ben withoutforth ben not
oures / but they that be wythin vs ben oures /
and therfore I haue receyued grete thynges of
god / for he hath made me lyke to his ymage /
He hath gyuen to me vnderftondyng / He hath
called me to his glorye / and hath opened to me
the yate of his kyngdom and therfor for thyfe
yeftes it is fyttyng to me to gyue hym prayf-
ynge / This yonge man feyng hyr prudence
axed of hir fader to haue hyr to wyf To whome
the

the fader fayd thou mayſt not haue my doughter /
for thou arte the ſone of ryche and noble kynne /
and I am but a poure man / but whan he ſore
deſyred hir / the olde man ſayd to hym / I may
not gyue hir to the ſyth thou wilt lede hir home
in to the hows of thy fader / for ſhe is myn
onelye daughter and haue no moo / And he
ſaid / I ſhal dwelle wyth thee and ſhal accorde
with the in al thynges / and thenne he dyd of
his precyous veſtements / and dyd on hym the
habyte of an olde man / and ſoo dwelling with
hym toke hir vnto his wyf and whan the olde
man had longe preuyd hym / he ladde hym in
to hys chambre / and ſhewyd to hym grete
plente of rycheſſes more than he euer had / and
gaue to hym al / & thenne Joſaphat ſayd to
hym / thys narracyon toucheth me couenably /
and I trowe thou haſt ſayd thys for me / Now
ſaye to me fader how many yere arte thou olde /
and where conuerſeſt thou / For fro the I wyl
neuer departe / To whom balaam ſayd / I haue
dwellyd xlv yere in the deſerte of the londe of
Sennaar / To whome Joſaphat ſayd / thou ſemeſt
better to be lxx yere / and he ſayd yf thou de-
maundeſt alle the yeres of my natyuyte / thou
haſt wel eſtemed them but I accounte not the
nombre of my lyf / them ſpecyally that I haue
dyſpended in the vanytee of the world / For I
was

was thenne dede toward god and I nombre not
the yerys of dethe / wyth the yerys of lyf / and
whan Jofaphat wold haue folowed hym in to
deferte balaam fayd to hym / yf thou do fo /
I fhal not haue thy companye / and I fhal be
thenne thanctor of perfecucyon to my brethern /
but whan thou feeft tyme couenable / thou fhalt
come to me / and thenne balaam baptyfed the
kynges fone / and enformed hym wel in the
feythe / and after retorned in to his celle / and a
lytel whyle after the kynge herde faye that hys
fone was cryftened / wherfore he was moche
forowful /· and one that was his frende named
Arachys recomfortyng hym fayd / Syr kynge I
knowe right well an olde hermyte that re-
fembleth moche balaam / and he is of our fecte /
He fhal fayne hym as he were balaam / & fhal
deffende fyrfte the feyth of cryften men / and
after fhal leue and retorne fro it / and thus your
fone fhal retorne to you / and thenne the kynge
wente in to deferte as it were to feche balaam
and toke thys hermyte and fayned that he had
taken balaam / and whan the kynges fone herde
that balaam was taken he wepte bytterlye / but
afterwarde he knewe by reuelacyon deuyne that
it was not he / ☙ Thenne the kynge wente to
his fone and fayd to hym thou haft put me in
grete heuyneffe / thou haft dyfhonoured myn
olde

olde age / thou haſt derked the light of myn eyen / ſone why haſt thou doon ſo / thou haſt forſaken the honour of my goddes and he anſwerd to hym I haue fledde the derkeneſſe / and am comen to the lyght / I haue fledde errour & knowe trouthe / and therfore trauaylle the for nought / for thou mayſt neuer wythdrawe me fro Jheſu cryſte / For lyke as it is Impoſſyble to the to touche the heuen wyth thy honde / or for to drye the grete ſee / ſo is it to the for to chaunge me / Thenne the fader ſayd / who is cauſe herof / but I my ſelf / that ſo gloryouſly haue to nouryſſhed the / that neuer fader nouriſſhed more hys ſone / For whyche cauſe thyn euyl wyll hath made the wood ageynſt me / and it is wel ryght / For the aſtronomyens in thy natyuyte ſayd / that thou ſholdeſt be proude and dyſhobedyente to thy parentes / but and thou now wylte not obeye me / thou ſhalte nomore be my ſone / and I ſhal be thyn enemye for a fader / and ſhal do to the that I neuer dyd to myn enemyes / To whome Joſaphat ſayd / fader wherfore arte thou angry / by cauſe I am made a partyner of good thynges / what fader was euer ſorowful in the proſperyte of hys ſone / I ſhal nomore calle the fader / but and yf thou be contrarye to me I ſhal flee the as a ſerpente /

            Thenne

Thenne the kynge departed from hym in grete angre / and fayd to arache his frende alle the hardnes of his fone and he counceylled the kynge that he fhold gyue hym noo fharpe wordes / for a chylde is better reformed by fayr and fwete wordes / The day folowyng the kynge came to his fone & beganne to clyppe enbrace and kyffe hym / and fayd to hym my ryght fwete fone honoure thou myn olde age / fone drede thy fader / knoweft thou not wel that it is good to obeye thy fader & make hym glad / and for to doo contrarye it is fynne / and they that angre them fynne euyl / to whome Jofaphat fayd there is tyme to loue / and tyme to hate / tyme of pees / and tyme of bataylle / and we ought in no wyfe loue them / ne obeye to them that wold put vs aweye fro god be it fader or moder /

And whan hys fader fawe his ftedfaftneffe / he fayd to hym / fythe I fee thy folye and wylte not obeye to me / Come and we fhal knowe the trouth / For balaam whiche hath deceyued the is bounden in my pryfon / and lete vs affemble our peple wyth balaam / and I fhal fende for alle the galylees / that they may faufly come wythout drede and dyfpute / and yf that ye with yon balaam ouercome vs / we fhal byleue and obeye you / and yf we
ouercome

ouercome you ye ſhal conſente to vs / and thys pleſyd wel to we kynge / and to Joſaphat / and whan they had ordeyned that he that named hym balaam ſhold fyrſte deffende the feythe of cryſte / And ſuffre hym after to be ouercomen and ſoo were all aſſemblyd / Thenne Joſaphat torned hym toward nachor whyche fayned hym to be balaam / and ſayd balaam thou knoweſt wel how thou haſte taughte me / and yf thou deffende the feyth that I haue lerned of the / I ſhal abyde in thy doctryne to the ende of my lyf / and yf thou be ouercomen I ſhal auenge me anone on the myn Iniurye / and ſhall plucke out the tonge out of thyn heed wyth myn handes / & gyue it to dogges to thende that thou be not ſo hardy to put a kynges ſone in errour /

And whan nachor herde that he was in grete fere and ſawe wel that yf he ſayd contrarye he were but dede / and that he was taken in his owne ſnare / and thenne he aduyſed that it were better to take and holde wyth the ſone thenne wyth the fader / For to eſchewe the perylle of deth / For the kynge had ſayd to hym tofore them all / that he ſhold deffende the feythe hardelye & without drede / thenne one of the mayſters ſayd to hym thou arte balaam / whiche haſt deceyued the ſone of the kynge / and he
ſayd

ſayd I am Balaam whyche haue not put the
kynges ſone in ony errour / but I haue broughte
hym out of errour / and thenne the mayſter
ſayd to hym / right noble and mearuyllous men
haue worſhypped our goddes / how dareſt thou
thenne adreſſe the ageynſt them / and he an-
ſwered / they of caldee / of egypte / and of
grece haue erryd and ſayden that the creatures
were goddes / & the chaldees ſuppoſeden that
the elementes had ben goddes whiche were
created to the prouffyte of men / and the
grekes ſuppoſed that curſyd men and tyrauntes
had be goddes / as ſaturne / whom they ſayd
ete his ſone / and Iubyter whiche as they ſay
gheldyd his fader & threwe his membrys in to
the ſee / wherof grewe venus / and Iubyter to
be kynge of the other goddes / by cauſe he
tranſformed ofte hym ſelf in lykeneſſe of a
beeſt / for to accomplyſhe his aduoultrye / and
alſo they ſaye that venus is goddeſſe of aduoultrye / and ſomtyme mars is hyr huſbond / and
ſomtyme adonydes / The egypcyens worſhyppe
the beeſtys / that is to wete a ſheep / a calfe /
a ſwyne / or ſuche other / and the cryſten men
worſhyppe the ſone of the ryght hyghe kynge /
that deſcended fro heuen and toke nature hu-
mayne /

And thenne nachor beganne clerelye to deffende

fende the lawe of cryſten men / & garnyſſhed hym wyth many reſons / ſo that the mayſters were al abaſſhed and wyſte not what to anſwere / and thenne Joſaphat had grete ioye of that / whiche our lord had deffended the trouthe / by hym that was enemye of trouthe / and thenne the kynge was ful of wodeneſſe / and commaunded that the counceyl ſhold departe / lyke as he wold haue tretyd ageyn on the morne the ſame fayte / Thenne Joſaphat ſayd to his fader lete my mayſter be wyth me thys nyght / to the ende that we may make our collacion to gyder / for to make to morowe our anſweres / and thou ſhalt lede thy mayſters wyth the / and ſhal take counceyl wyth them / & yf thou lede my mayſter wyth the / thou doeſt me no ryghte / wherfore he graunted to hym nachor by cauſe he hoped that he ſhold deceyue hym / and whan the kynges ſone was comen to his chambre / and nachor with hym / Joſaphat ſayd to nachor / Ne weneſt thou not that I knowe the / I wote wel that thou arte not balaam / but thou arte nachor the aſtronomyen / and Joſaphat prechyd thenne to hym the waye of helthe / and conuertyd hym to the feythe / and on the morne ſente hym in to deſerte / and there was baptyſed / and ledde the lyf of an hermyte / Thenne there was an enchauntour

enchauntour named theodas / whan he herde of this thynge / he came to the kyng and fayd that he fhold make his fone retorne and byleue in hys goddes /

And the kyng faid to hym yf thou do fo / I fhal make to the an ymage of golde and offre facrefyfes therto / lyke as to my goddes / and he fayd take aweye al them that ben about thy fone and put to hym fayre wymmen and wel adourned / and commaunde them alle waye to abyde by hym / and after I fhal fende a wycked fpyryte that fhal enflamme hym to luxurye / and there is noo thynge that may fo fone deceyue the yonge men / as the beaulte of wymmen / and he fayd yet more / there was a kynge whyche had wyth grete payne a fone / & the wyfe mayfters fayden that yf he fawe fonne or mone wythin ten yere / he fhold lofe the fyghte of his eyen /

Thenne hit was ordeyned that thys chylde fhold be nourifhed wythin a pytte made in a grete rocke / and whan the ten yere were paffyd / The kynge commaunded that hys fone fhold be brought forth and that all thynges fhold be broughte tofore hym by caufe he fhold knowe the names and the thynges / and thenne they brought tofore hym Jewelles / horfes and beeftys of al names / and alfo golde /
fyluer

fyluer precyous ftones / & all other thynges and
whan he had demaūded the names of euery
thynge / and that the mynyftres had tolde hym /
he fette nought therby / and whan his fader
faw that he retched not of fuche thynges /
thene the kynge made to be broughte tofore
hym wymmen quayntely arayed / and he demaunded what they were / For they wold not
foo lyghtly telle hym / wherof he was anoyed /
and after the mayfter fquyer of the kyng fayd
iapyng that they were deuylles that deceyue
men / Thenne the kynge demaunded hym what
he lyeueft had of al that he had feen / and he
anfweryd fader my foule coueyteth noo thynge
fo moche as the deuylles that deceyue men /
and therfore I fuppofe that none other thynge
fhal furmounte thy fone but wymmen whiche
moeue men alle waye to lecherye / thenne the
kynge put out alle his mynyftres and fette
therin to be about his fone riȝt noble & fayre
maydens / whyche alweye hym admonefted to
playe / and there were none other that myght
fpeke ne ferue hym / and anone the enchauntour fent to hym the deuyl for to enflame
hym whiche brennyd the yonge man wythinforth / & the maydens wythoutforth / and whan
he felte hym foo ftrongelye trauaylled he was
moche angry / and recommaunded hym felf
alle

alle to god / and he receyued deuyne comforte / in fuche wyfe that al temptacyon departed from hym / & after this that the kynge fawe that the deuyl had don no thynge he fente to hym a fayre mayden a kynges doughter whyche was faderles / To whome this man of god prechyd and fhe anfwerd yf thou wylte faue me / and take me aweye fro worfhyppyng of thy dolles / conioyne the vnto me by couplyng of maryage / for the patryarkes / prophetes / and peter the appoftle had wyues / and he fayd to hir / woman thyfe wordes fayeft thou now for nought / It apperteyneth wel to cryften men to wedde wyues / but not to them that haue promyfed to our lord to kepe vyrgynyte /

And fhe fayd to hym / now be it as thou wylte / but yf thou wylte faue my fowle / graunte to me a lytel requefte / lye wyth me onelye this nyght and I promyfe to the that to morne I fhal be made cryften / For as ye fay the aungels have more ioye in heuen of one fynnar doyng penaunce / thenne on many other / There is grete guerdon due to hym that doth penaunce / & conuerteth hym / therfore graunte to me onely thys requefte / and foo thou fhalte faue me / and thenne fhe began ftrongely to affayle the toure of hys confcience / Thenne the deuyl fayd to his felowes / loo fee
how

how this mayde hath ſtrongely put forth that we myȝt not moeue / Come thenne and lete vs knocke ſtrongely ageynſt hym ſyth we fynde now tyme couenable /

And whan the holy yonge man ſawe thys thynge / and that he was in that caytyfnes / That the couetyſe of hys fleſſhe admoneſted hym to ſynne /

And alſo that he deſyred the ſauacyon of the mayde / by entyſyng of the deuyl that moeuyd hym / he thenne put hym ſelf to prayer in wepynge / and there fyl a ſlepe / and ſawe by a vyſyon that he was broughte in to a medowe arayed wyth fayr floures / there where the leuys of the trees demened a ſwete ſounde / whiche came by a wynde agreable / and therout yſſued a merueyllous odour / and the fruyte was right fayre to ſee / and right delectable of taſte / and there were ſetes of golde and ſyluer and precyous ſtones / and the beddes were noble and precyouſly adurned / and ryght clere water ranne there by / and after that he entred in to a cyte of which the walles were of fyne golde / and ſhone by meruayllous clereneſſe / and ſawe in the ayer ſomme that ſange a ſonge / that neuer eer of mortal man herde lyke / and it was ſayd this is the place of bleſſyd ſayntes / and as they wolde haue had hym thens / he prayed them that
thēy

they wold lete hym dwelle there and they fayd
to hym / thou fhalte yet hereafter come hyther
wyth grete trauayle yf thou mayſt ſuffre / and
after they ledde hym in to a ryght horryble
place ful of al fylthe and ſtenche / and fayd to
hym this is the place of wycked peple / and
whan he awoke hym femed that the beaute of
that damoyfel was more foull and ſtynkyng
thenne alle the other ordure / and thenne the
wycked fpyrytes came ageyn to theodafe / and
he thenne blamyd them / to whome they fayd
we ranne vpon hym tofore he marked wyth
the fygne of the croſſe / & troubled hym ſtronge-
lye and whan he was garnyſſhed with the fygne
of the croſſe / he perſecuted vs by grete force /
Thenne theodafe came to hym with the kynge
and had hoped that he ſhold haue peruerted
hym / But this enchauntour was taken of hym /
whome he ſuppoſed to haue taken and was
conuerted and receyued baptefme / and lyued
after an holy lyf and thenne the kynge was
al defpayred / and by counceyl of his frendes
he delyuered to hym halfe his royame / &
how be it that Jofaphat defyred wyth alle his
thoughte the deferte / yet for to encrece the
feythe he receyued the royame for a certeyn
tyme / and maad chirches and reyfed croffes
and conuerted moche people of his royame to
the

the fayth of Jhesu cryste / and atte last the fader consented to the resons & predycacions of his sone and byleuyd on the feythe of Jhesu cryst / & receyued baptesme / and lefte his royame hole to his sone / & entended to werkes of penaunce / and after fynysshed hys lyf laudably / and Josaphat ofte warned the kyng barachye that he wolde goo in to deserte / but he was reteyned of the peple longe tyme / but atte laste he fledde aweye in to deserte / and as he wente in a deserte / he gafe to a pour man his habyte ryal / and abode in a ryght pour gowne / & the deuyl made to hym many assaultes / for somtyme he ranne vpon hym wyth a swerde drawen / and menaced to smyte yf he lefte not the deserte / and another tyme he apperyd to hym in the forme of a wylde beest / & fomed & ranne on hym as he wold haue deuoured hym / and thenne Josaphat sayd / Our Lord is myn helpar / I doubte no thynge that man may do to me / and thus Josaphat was two yere vagaunte & erryd in deserte / and coude not fynde balaam and at the laste he fonde a caue in the erthe and knockyd at the dore & sayd / Fader blesse me / and anone balaam herde the voys of hym / and roos vp & wente out / and thenne eche kyssed other and enbraced straytelye / and were glad of their
assemblyng /

aſſemblyng / and after Joſaphat recounted to balaam al thyſe thynges that were happenyd /

And he rendryd & gaue thankynges to god therfore / and Joſaphat dwelled there many yeres in grete and meruayllous penaunce ful of vertues / and whan balaam had accomplyſſhed hys dayes / he reſtyd in pees aboute the yere of our lord foure hondred & four ſcore Joſaphat lefte his royame the xxv yere of his age / and ledde the lyf of an hermyte fyue and thyrty yere / and thenne reſtyd in pees ful of vertues / and was buryed by the body of balaam / and whan the kyngs barachyas herde of thys thynge he came vnto that ſame place with a grete companye / and toke the bodyes and bare them wyth moche grete honoure in to hys cytee where god hath ſhewed many fayre myracles at the tombe of thyſe two precyous bodyes /

℞ **Thus endeth the ſtory of balaam and Joſaphat.**

THE POWER of ALMIGHTY GOD,

SET FORTH IN THE

Heathen's Converſion;

Shewing the Whole

LIFE

OF

Prince JEHOSAPHAT,

The SON of

KING AVENERIO,

Of BARMA in INDIA.

IN SEVEN PARTS.

How he was converted and made a Chriſtian, which was the converſion of his Father and the whole Land.

By a Reverend DIVINE.

LONDON:

Printed in the Year 1783.

Price TWO-PENCE.

THE POWER of ALMIGHTY GOD,

Set forth in the

HEATHENS CONVERSION.

PART I.

King Avenerio's *Perfecution over the Chriftian Faith; he prayeth to his Idols that his Queen might bear a Child.*

Which may be fung to the tune, Aim not too high.

GOOD Chriftian people, now be pleas'd to mind,
This pious book, and in it foon you'll find,
Divine records fhow plainly to our view,
What miracles our gracious God can do.
 Full well we know this is the heathens cafe,
Tho' they have not receiv'd the light of grace:
By nature the fun, moon, and ftars obey,
Thus every land fome kind of homage pay.

Thus

Thus by degrees God calls them home we know,
And mighty miracles does daily ſhow,
To make his righteous goſpel ſpread and ſhine,
That all may know his power moſt divine.

Then let the ignorant atheiſt bluſh for ſhame,
And never more abuſe God's holy name,
For God created all things, great and ſmall,
And man to be chief ruler over all.

The cauſe of this my treating I'll explain,
In foreign lands a tyrant KING did reign;
A perſecutor of the chriſtian faith,
As many good and learned writers ſaith.

His Queen was young and beautiful alſo,
In worldly pleaſures they did overflow;
One thing which moſt their comforts did deſtroy,
They had no iſſue that could it enjoy.

This King, who in vain idols did believe,
Sent for his prieſts to pray ſhe might conceive;
Pray to our Gods, ſaid he, that we may have,
A child for that is all I need to crave.

For with all ſorts of plenty I am bleſt,
What e'er my heart can wiſh to be poſſeſt:
A child will crown my days with pleaſure then,
And I ſhould be the happieſt of all men.

They all replied, we will your will obey,
And for this thing we to our Gods will pray:
The King ſaid, if ſuch bleſſings come to me,
Then you ſhall ſurely well rewarded be.

Vain

Vain ignorant man God's laws fo difobey'd,
To think that idols, which by hands are made,
Have power; no; fuch things let us defy,
And put our faith and truft in God moft high.
   Who is the righteous living God of might,
Nothing is hidden from his bleffed fight,
He knows man's thoughts, and fees his actions ftill,
And nothing can be done without his will.

PART II.

The Queen proving with Child, he rewarded his Idol Priefts, and fent for the Wife Men.

THUS in a vain prefumptuous manner, they,
   Did often to their golden idols pray,
According to the order of their King,
Which was indeed a bold prefumptuous thing.
   From heathen priefts no virtue could proceed,
But by the work of God it was decreed,
His fond defire fhould fulfilled be,
That he a mighty miracle fhould fee.
   According to the will of God above,
His Queen conceived, and with child did prove,
Then did the King joy through the land proclaim,
And thought his idol Gods had caus'd the fame.

Unto

Unto his heathen priefts great gifts he fent,
Saying, my days are crowned with fweet content:
My Queen has now conceived, and I fhall have,
The thing which I fo long did wifh and crave.

Five of the wifeft men that could be found,
In King Avenerio's kingdom round,
He fent for them and did a feaft prepare,
Three months before her time expired were.

Unto thefe wife philofophers he faid,
My Queen in three months will be brought to bed;
'Till then, you in my palace fhall remain,
That I may know what planet then will reign.

PART III.

The Queen being delivered of JEHOSAPHAT, the Wife Men tell the Signification of the Child's Planet.

AT laft fhe was delivered of a fon,
    Which joyful tidings thro' the kingdom run,
The fweeteft child that ever eyes beheld,
With joy and gladnefs then the King was filled.

JEHOSAPHAT this prince was nam'd we find:
The wife men were difturbed in their minds,
                                    For

For by the rule of planets they did see,
Such things as would not with the King agree.
    Four of them said, what shall we do alas!
For thro' this child strange things will come to pass;
Therefore we must dissemble with our King,
And tell him, 'twill be well in every thing.
    Now when the wise men came in the King's view!
He said, what have you found, pray tell me true?
Four of them said, fortune has on you smil'd,
For you are blest with a sweet hopeful child.
    In every thing he will obey your will,
And crown your days with joy and comfort still:
To hear these things the King was pleased in mind;
The wisest man he fear'd, and staid behind.
    Then from the King these wise men did depart:
He for the other sent, and said, thou art
The wisest man, and therefore tell thou me,
What you concerning of my child did see?
    I am afraid to tell you, he reply'd,
Because, O King! you'll be dissatisfied;
Let it be good, or ill, speak, said the King,
For thee I will believe in every thing.
    He said, O King! those men did flatter you;
What they have said, indeed it is not true:

                                            For

For in that fatal hour I did fee,
Your child is born a chriftian for to be.

   Up firmly for the chriftian faith he'll ftand,
And all your priefts he'll banifh from the land;
Your golden Gods he clearly will deftroy;
Your days are mix'd with grief inftead of joy.

   Hearing thefe words the King to weeping fell,
Saying, this is fad news which now you tell,
My joys are turn'd to forrow, grief and woe,
Then how I may prevent it, let me know.

   The wife philofopher then faid, behold,
Your child muft fuck till three years old,
And build a famous palace in that fpace,
That he may be fecured in that place.

   To wait on him, get twelve young virgins fair,
And fome great knight to tutor him with care,
The word of God or Chrift ne'er let him hear,
And thus let him be kept for fifteen years.

   Should one of them fall fick, or chance to die,
Be fure you get another fpeedily;
No death or ficknefs let him e'er perceive,
But all for ever lives, make him believe.

   Then take him forth all pleafures for to fee,
And to fome princefs let him wedded be:
By this contrivance I'll affure you true,
Your child will be a comfort unto you.

PART

PART IV.

King AVENERIO's contrivance to have his son brought up in the Heathen Way, which prevailed not.

THEN as the wife philosopher had said,
    He caused a sumptuous palace to be made,
And soon he got twelve virgins as we hear,
All aged from thirteen unto twenty years.

    He put in trust Lionone called by name,
Who was a noble baron of great fame,
That he might be his tutor, and his guide,
To learn him well, and train him up in pride.

    He was to be confined for fifteen years,
Commanding that God's word he might not hear,
Nor any talk of holy things divine;
But mark how God did baulk the King's design.

    His father came oft times to see him there,
To whom the tutor——did this declare,
Your son he doth increase in learning so,
He'll be a wise philosopher I know.

    Then said the King, the wise man told to me,
My child was born a christian for to be;
That false philosopher I need not mind,
For now I shall much joy and comfort find.

    When 12 long years were gone and past behold,
The prince was then about fifteen years old;

He lov'd one virgin more than all the reft,
To whom Jehofaphat his mind expreft.
 Why am I fo confined here, I pray?
I long to fee my father's palace gay,
And walk abroad to take the air likewife,
Why are thefe things thus hidden from my eyes.
 Now if you will reveal the truth to me,
Thou ever fhalt high in my favour be;
But if thou doft refufe, I'll fcorn thee quite,
And never will endure thee in my fight.
 The damfel faid, then as her eyes did flow,
Your father will put me to death I know,
If I fhould tell; and if I it refufe,
Then I for ever muft your favour lofe.
 Jehofaphat faid, fpeak, be not afraid:
So then fhe told him what the wife men faid;
And did unto the prince the caufe relate,
Why he was kept confined at this rate.
 Should you go forth, the city for to fee,
Your heart with mirth will ravifh'd be,
To view the court, and famous buildings ftore,
This fet the prince a longing more and more.
 And faid to Lionone, one thing I crave,
To walk abroad I may fome freedom have:
The knight went to the King, and got him leave,
But, O the King in floods of tears did grieve.
 The King fet forth a proclamation then,
That blind and lame, and all deformed men,
Should

Should keep up close when as the prince past thro',
But strong and lusty should appear in view.

 The prince was mounted on a lofty steed,
Great lords and barons met him there indeed,
To 'commodate him through the city fair,
While at each window music play'd most rare.

 The people were amaz'd at this fine sight,
Likewise the prince was fill'd with great delight;
Then home he went, and to the damsel told,
What pleasant sights that day he did behold.

 Most royal prince, the damsel then did say,
Did you but see the fields and gardens gay,
Where birds do sing, and fragrant flowers grow,
You would be much more ravished I know.

 Once more the tutor did the King acquaint,
The second time to give his son content:
Setting his proclamation forth again,
So out they went with all their noble train.

 The fields and gardens gave him great delight,
And singing birds his heart did much invite;
He was well pleas'd to view the parks most rare,'
When evening come, for home they did repair.

 But now to drive off all these pleasures gay,
They met with two objects by the way:
One blind, the other full of leprosy,
Who for the sake of God crav'd charity.

The

The prince unto his tutor then did say,
What is the meaning, tell me now I pray,
Of these strange creatures? straight the knight
    replies,
They are two Men full of infirmities.

  For by the cause of sin 'tis God's decree,
Some men are born afflicted for to be;
As blind or lame, such things the Lord doth
    show,
That all may praise his name who are not so.

  Jehosaphat then said, If this be true,
The like as well may fall on me or you,
The Knight then said God knows best, so home
    they went,
Jehosaphat was fill'd with discontent.

  The Tutor then unto the King made known,
Your son is very melancholy grown,
Some sport and pastime therefore let him see,
In hopes his drooping heart may cheered be.

  The King gave leave, the tutor once more
    came
With many lords and barons of great fame,
To ride a hunting then they took their way,
In mirth they spent a pleasant summer's day.

  But riding home, out of a cell appears
A man whose age was near an hundred years,
Bald-headed, toothless, hollow-ey'd withal,
The palsy shook him, he could hardly crawl;
                                Jehosaphat

Jehofaphat then faid, Pray let me know
What thing is this fo ftrange and feems to go?
The Knight faid 'tis a man with age quite fpent,
Ready to die,——this made the prince relent.
Prince.) When muft he die, O tell me now I pray?
Tutor.) No one but God can tell his dying day.
Pr.) What muft be done with him when he is dead?
Tu.) Then under earth his body muft be laid.
   Then said the prince, If that it muft be fo,
This is a vain deceitful world I know,
The pleafures of it I'll no longer prize,
But have the thoughts of death before mine eyes.
   Now when the tutor had thefe things then told,
The King did weep, and faid, my heart feems cold,
My child is come to ruin now, alas!
I fear the wife man's words will come to pafs.

PART V.

Prince Jehofaphat's Converfion to the Chriftian Faith and Doctrine.

BARLAAM, a chriftian hermit, who had fpent
    Long time in defert places, to him God fent
An angel, who unto the hermit faith,
Go teach Jehofaphat the chriftian faith.
                            Whate'er

Whate'er thou fayeft he fhall be rul'd by thee;
For God hath chofe Jehofaphat to be
His faithful fervant, guiltlefs of offence,
Tho' kept fo long in wicked ignorance.
    Then Barlaam came unto the palace brave,
To whom the porter faid, what would you have?
Said Barlaam, I muft fpeak with your great
    prince.
The man at firft deny'd him entrance.
    Barlaam.) I am a merchant, now I tell to thee,
And bring a precious jewel here with me,
All other things the fame it doth outvie,
For he who keeps the fame fhall never die.
    The virtue of this jewel is fo pure,
All manner of diftempers it will cure:
If he were blind 'twould give him perfect fight,
If he were lame 'twould make him walk upright.
    Porter.) Pray let me fee this jewel if you can?
Barlaam.) I dare not fhow it to a married man,
For none muft fee it but a virgin pure,
Your prince a virgin is I can affure.
    The porter knowing what he faid was true,
Said, I will go and tell the prince of you:
He went and told the prince, who foon was free
He to his chamber fhould admitted be.
    When Barlaam came the prince faid Let me
    fee
The precious jewel you have brought for me.
Barlaam

Barlaam.) You cannot see it with an outward
   sight,
But must behold it with an inward light.
   Then Prince Jehosaphat did mildly say,
What do you mean by inward light I pray?
Barlaam the hermit made this answer then,
This jewel is the *Saviour of all men.*
   The gods you serve are devils I you tell,
And leading you the ready way to hell;
There's none to serve but one true God of
   Might,
Hearken to me and I will teach you right.
   God made the heavens, Lucifer first fell
With many more down to the pit of hell,
For pride, and so the devils all became
To be tormented in a burning flame.
   Those having fell, the heavens were left bare,
So by that means the worlds created were;
In six days space God did this work fulfil,
And make all things according to his will:
   Man being made well-pleasing in his sight,
The devil was enrag'd with wrath and spight,
'Cause he himself can in no pleasure dwell,
He fain would draw all souls to him in hell.
   The devil's snare first caused Adam's fall,
Which was the cause mankind have sinned all,
And so the world became filthy and vain,
But by Christ's death it was restor'd again.

When

D

When Barlaam had explain'd the scripture
    o'er,
The prince increas'd in learning more and more:
He said, I will believe and bear in mind
My Christ that dy'd for me and all mankind.
    O teach me how to serve my God most pure,
That after death my soul may be secure,
With God & Christ who dwells with the Most
    High,
Barlaam in parable made this reply:
    To a great lord two coffins once were brought,
One of them very fine and richly wrought
With gold, the other rotten were,
He chose that coffin which was wrought so rare:
    The gaudy coffin being open'd wide,
A parcel of old rotten bones he spy'd;
The rotten coffin then burst open were,
Where he beheld choice pearls and di'monds
    rare:
    He blusht for shame and was converted straight,
Crying, O Lord, my sins are very great;
The glory of the earth is vain I see,
The poorest of this earth will happiest be.
    The prince said I will worldly pleasure slight,
And in the poor will place my whole delight;
Henceforth I will defy all pomp and pride,
I thank you brother, Jesus be my guide.

PART VI.

King Avenerio's Malice against his Son Jehosaphat for being a Christian.

LIONONE finding what would come to pass,
    He smote upon his breast, and cry'd alas
What answer shall I make my sovereign lord?
Death without mercy will be my reward.
  Then he a rope about his neck did fling,
And in this manner went unto the king,
Then kneeling down he made a courteous bow,
The king reply'd, sir, what's the matter now?
  What, art thou mad, Lionone, tell me true,
That you appear so strangely in my view?
Lionone trembled; and made this reply,
O hang me up, for I deserve to die.
  I do deserve no mercy for my share,
You left your son under my charge and care,
To tutor him the way that is most right,
But now, alas! your son is turned quite.
  For by a false deceitful man's advice,
Who said he had a jewel of great price:
By his sly ways I fell into a snare;
He's made your son a christian I declare.
  He in the christian faith is grown so bold,
That our religion he in scorn doth hold:

He

He rails againſt our Gods at a vile rate,
And ſays they ſhall be burned at his gate.
 Riſe up Lionone, then replied the King,
I will not execute you for this thing:
Thou may'ſt be ſure no harm ſhall come to thee,
But on my ſon revenged I will be.
 If that he will not turn to us again,
As I'm King, I'll cauſe him to be ſlain:
I'd better kill him though he is my child,
Than let my kingdom utterly be ſpoil'd.
 So ſending for his ſon theſe words he ſaid,
Haſt thou my laws and counſel diſobey'd?
If it be true what I have heard of thee,
Then by my honour thou deſtroy'd ſhalt be.
 I have been told thou art a chriſtian turn'd,
If it be ſo, 'tis fit thou ſhould'ſt be burn'd:
Thou ſhalt not live to overcome my land,
The truth of this now let me underſtand.
 Father I am a chriſtian to be plain,
That holy faith I ever will maintain:
To ſuffer death I will be very free,
For my dear Chriſt that ſhed his blood for me.
 Then did he give his ſon ſad kicks and blows,
'Till blood guſht out both from his mouth and noſe.
I thank you, Father, then replied the ſon,
It is God's will for me, this ſhould be done.

My

My ſaviour Chriſt with many ſtripes was beat,
And to the croſs they nail'd his hands and feet,
To bear your blows with patience I am free,
I cannot bear what Chriſt has bore for me.

To find out Barlaam then we underſtand,
He ſent a proclamation through the land;
That man by whom this hermit could be found,
Should have for his reward a hundred pound.

Long time they ſought him, but 'twas in vain,
He thought to take his ſon, and have him ſlain,
His council ſaid, your ſon pray do not ſlay,
And we will put you in a better way.

Nicor reſembles Barlaam in the face,
Let him be brought before his royal grace,
He'll think 'tis Barlaam, therefore Nicor muſt,
Tell him the heathen way is good and juſt.

And ſay 'twas falſe what he had ſaid before,
So by that means your ſon we may reſtore;
And bring him ſafe into our way again,
Then he the chriſtian faith will quite diſdain.

Let all the chriſtians which confined are,
Be brought into your royal palace rare,
To hear the ſtrong diſpute; when this is done,
They'll all turn heathens with the prince your ſon.

Then Nicor being ſent for to the court,
The King unto his ſon gave this report:

Barlaam

Barlaam is taken which thou foon fhalt fee,
Then faid the prince, this news rejoiceth me.

So foon as Nicor to the court was brought,
The prince was filled with a jealous thought,
It was not Barlaam, fometimes he thought he was,
Then he began to plead the heathen's caufe.

The prince before them all, faid, wicked elf,
What art thou come to plead againft thyfelf?
Except thou doft the chriftian faith maintain,
This very day by me thou fhalt be flain.

Remember David, God anointed King,
Who flew the proud Philiftines with a fling:
If thou art ne'er fo ftrong, affured I be,
Into my hands God will deliver thee.

Said Nicor, I was fent you to deceive,
The Devil brought me here I do believe:
I am not Barlaam, Nicor is my name,
Brought up a heathen lord, the more's my fhame.

No more I'll be a heathen for my part,
But ferve the chriftian God with all my heart:
The pagans down their heathen books did fling
And burnt their Gods in prefence of the King.

PART

PART VII.

The conversion of King Avenerio, which caused the gospel of Christ to be publicly manifested throughout the whole land.

SEEING these things the King aloud did cry
   O! what a wretched sinful man am I?
Against the holy word of truth to fight,
I find the christian faith is pure and right.
   Against that faith I will no longer hold:
O blessed be the wise men that foritold,
What was degreed at the sweet righteous birth,
The blessed'st child that ere was born on earth:
   Dear son, behold I fall down at thy feet,
Hoping thou wilt by prayer to God intreat
In my behalf to cleanse my sinful soul,
Which has been long polluted vain and foul.
   Rise up dear father, then the prince did say,
I'll beg of God to wash your sins away.
My heart is cheer'd to see such change in you,
The thoughts do more and more my joys renew.
   Father, it was God's will I should be sent
To save you from the dreadful punishment
Of hell's hot fire which does poor souls destroy,
We shall be crown'd with everlasting joy.
   Churches were built——the land became divine,
Then did the righteous gospel spread and shine;

The poor confined christians were set free,
In christian love the land did soon agree.

    Death call'd the king down to his silent tomb,
Jehosaphat reigned in his father's room,
And was by all his subjects dearly lov'd
Because the word of Christ was well approv'd.

    Thus for some time he did the faith defend,
But in that land his life he did not end;
But to Alfanes did his throne resign,
That he might keep it holy and divine.

    For fear that worldly pleasures which are vain
In any wife should draw him back again,
He sought out Barlaam to be satisfy'd,
In lonesome deserts he with hermits dy'd.

    The people griev'd for loss of their good prince.
But good Alfanes stood in the defence
Of the true faith, which is divine and pure,
And ever shall from age to age endure.

    All we who in a christian nation dwell
Should mind God's word, and prize it very well
And not abuse it as we daily do,
For fear just punishment should us pursue.

    Since mighty miracles so plain are seen,
Let's beg of God for faith to make us clean;
That after death our souls may live on high
With JESUS CHRIST to all Eternity.

F I N I S.

www.ingramcontent.com/pod-product-compliance
Lightning Source LLC
Chambersburg PA
CBHW032149160426
43197CB00008B/830